D0994350

Gazza Agonistes

Gazza Agonistes

IAN HAMILTON

BLOOMSBURY

First published in Great Britain 1998

Copyright © 1998 by Ian Hamilton

The moral right of the author has been asserted

Bloomsbury Publishing Plc, 38 Soho Square, London WIV 5DF

A CIP catalogue record for this book
is available from the British Library

ISBN 0 7475 4152 3

10 9 8 7 6 5 4 3 2 1

Typeset by Hewer Text Ltd, Edinburgh
Printed in Great Britain by Clays Limited, St Ives plc

Contents

Prefatory Note

T HE BULK OF this book first appeared in 1994, under the title *Gazza Italia*. Its first appearance, though, was as an article in *Granta* magazine, where it was called *Gazza Agonistes*, a much better title, in my view. I have added to the original a lengthy postscript, bringing the action up to date and I have made a few small changes to the *Gazza Italia* text. I have been sparing, though, with hindsight. After all, this is a fan's eye-view of Paul Gascoigne – and fans, as we know, are expert at reassembling dashed hopes.

Newcastle

M Y FIRST SIGHTING of Paul Gascoigne was in 1987, when he was playing for Newcastle. I didn't exactly fall for him that day but I certainly looked twice. There was, as they say, 'something about him'. His giftedness was self-evident: he was a natural. You could tell that from his touch. However the ball came at him, fast, medium or slow, he welcomed it; he took it in his stride.

His appearance was unprepossessing. He was plump, twitchy and pink-faced, and on the small side. And he was cheeky in a puerile sort of way. He was always looking to nutmeg defenders when it would have been easier to pass them by. He wanted the ball *all the time*: for throw-ins, free kicks, corners – goal-kicks, if they had let him. He seemed fragile but he wasn't: there was a mean streak underneath the puppy fat. He was always glancing behind him, or from side to side, even when the ball was nowhere near. He talked a lot, played to the crowd, or tried to. At nineteen, Gascoigne came across as a trainee star, a star whose moment was – well, any second now.

I was intrigued by the way he related to his centre forward, a Brazilian called Mirandinha. Mirandinha had not long before scored for Brazil against England at Wembley, and when Newcastle signed him there had been a small fuss in the press. Wags said that the Newcastle board thought they were signing Maradona. For the most part, though, the appearance of a Brazilian in our English league was seen as a matter for great celebration. We would learn from Mirandinha. He would bring sunshine to our drizzly field of play.

What he actually brought was a repertoire of muttered curses and black looks, and in the game I watched most of them were directed at young Gascoigne – who was, in theory, his midfield supplier. The supply, it must be said, rarely arrived. When Mirandinha was unmarked, Gascoigne tended to ignore him, preferring instead to set off on an intricate, inventive and usually doomed run into the heart of the enemy's defence. When Mirandinha *was* marked, or merely unavailable, Gascoigne liked to zip classy first-time balls into spaces where the Brazilian should have been, but never was. For much of the game, Newcastle's exotic foreigner was to be seen standing in the opposition's eighteen-yard box, hands on hips, eyes raised in exasperation to the heavens. Sunshine he was not.

Was the bumptious youth taking a rise out of his illustrious team-mate? Certainly Mirandinha seemed to think so. Midway through the second half, after yet another chance had failed to come his way, he strode over to Gascoigne and said something, something indignant, to judge from the arm-waving that went with it. And Gascoigne simply gaped back at him, as if to say: what *is* this? What have I done wrong? Why aren't you pleased with me?

And it was then, I think, that I began to wonder about this funny-looking kid, began to think he might be special.

Gascoigne had not, I decided, been trying to make a monkey out of Mirandinha. On the contrary: he'd been trying to *impress* him, as one Brazilian, one artist, to another, young to old. And now, chastised for his selfishness, he was forlorn, perplexed. I don't think Gascoigne touched the ball again that afternoon. Mirandinha maybe got his goal, from someone else's pass; I can't recall. In any case, he never scored that many and was shortly on his way back to Brazil.

Was Gascoigne actually perplexed, or was he putting it all on? Or was he cast down because his virtuoso stuff had not come off? What if it *had* come off – as so often it so nearly did? Would he then have told the fuming Mirandinha where to go, told him he wasn't the only, perhaps not even the *real*, Brazilian in the team? He might well have done. For all his appearance of naughty-boy bewilderment, Gascoigne's cockiness probably ran just as deep, was just as fierce, as Mirandinha's pride. But then there was the sulk, the opting out. What did this signify? I noticed that, after his rebuke, Gascoigne started to make strange, spasmodic head movements and began muttering to himself. He kept licking his lips, flexing his jaw muscles, tucking his shirt in, pulling up his socks. And his face turned a more brilliant shade of pink. At the whistle, though, as the teams were walking from the field, he was immediately at Mirandinha's side, chattering and joking, linking arms, the best of friends. And the Brazilian's noble scowl seemed to be softening: perhaps this boy-man means no harm.

All this, I am aware, sounds fanciful and is perhaps misremembered, written up. But if it is, well, that is the spectator's fate – we watch but in the end we have to guess. What I do know is that this was the day on which I became a

Gascoigne fan-in-waiting, or in-hope. And it so happened that I rather badly needed a new soccer hero: Glenn Hoddle, my fixation for the past ten years, was on the wane. His admirers had grown weary of their long campaign to get his genius established in the England team. After his error against Russia in the European Nations Cup, we knew that the England manager at the time, Bobby Robson, would not pick him again. Jimmy Greaves was, of course, long gone. Steve Archibald had never quite shaped up. Richard Gough was a defender. All of these heroes used to play for Tottenham Hotspur. Was it possible for me to be smitten by a footballer who didn't play for Spurs? And was this Gascoigne true hero material? It seemed unlikely, but we'd see. So far, I told myself, we hadn't seen enough.

It helped, though, that Gascoigne was a Geordie. I had grown up in the North-East and I could just about recall the great days of Jackie Milburn and Bobby Mitchell, Cup winners three times in the 1950s. The black-and-white stripes had meant nothing much down south for thirty years, but for me they still had glamour. And I could remember the fervour, the near-desperation, of those Geordie fans. If Gascoigne did come good, became a Beardsley or a Waddle, the gratitude of Tyneside would be his.

Or would it? At that first game, the fans had seemed equivocal. A certain amount of dour North-Eastern grumbling could be heard: ponce, fairy and the like. But at Tottenham they said this kind of thing about Glenn Hoddle from time to time: it was an aspect of their adoration. Newcastle fans are different, though. They have been badly used; their adoration is *always* coloured with distrust. If Gascoigne did turn out to be as good as they wanted him to be, he would almost certainly be sold. What they really yearned for was a star who would be theirs for keeps and help them to win something big: a Jackie Milburn. Deep down they knew that there was not much chance of *that*.

Most soccer fans have a need to get hooked on the fortunes of a single player, to build a team around him, so to speak. When England played well without Hoddle, I took a diminished pleasure in their triumph. What it chiefly signified to me, and to my co-worshippers, was that Glenn would not be in the team next time. On the other hand, if Glenn *had* played, had made the winning goal, our patriotic joy would have been boundless. Even at Tottenham, where my engagement really was supposed to encompass the whole team, victories were not complete unless Hoddle had had a significant hand in them. And it was much the same with Jimmy Greaves. How many Greaves fans, I wonder, wholeheartedly savoured that 1966 World Cup win? Greaves didn't. He left the stadium immediately after the presentations and skipped the banquet afterwards. How could we not skip it too?

I like to think that to be this kind of fan you have to be part yob, part connoisseur. To appreciate Hoddle's vision and finesse you need to have rare powers of discrimination. To fret for hours about whether or not he will do the business against Kuwait you need to be short of something else to think about. I also like to pretend that such a fan must be equipped with unusual qualities of loyalty, persistence and fortitude in the face of accumulating set-backs. With a pop star or an opera singer, when you turn up for a performance, you usually get more or less what you go to see, or hear. With soccer heroes, there is no such guarantee, or even likelihood: each performance is a new ordeal; the better the performer, the more determined the other side to stop him doing what he's good at. The odds against get higher all the time.

I remember once taking an American friend along to Tottenham's White Hart Lane to watch Jimmy Greaves. This player, I announced beforehand, is the best, simply the best: just wait and see. Greaves barely got a kick all afternoon. He was marked ferociously, man for man, or men for man. More than once he was hacked down just as he was about to set off on one of his legendary scampers towards the goal. After a few tumbles, he evidently decided that this was not to be his day. He slowed down, drifted here and there and altogether did the minimum – which, it has to be confessed, he was (also) quite good at. At one point, my companion was mystified to observe Greaves in the centre circle, idly chatting to the opposition's centre half, the most effective of his markers. Spurs, in the meantime, were under serious pressure at the other end.

It was at moments like this that the yob in me ('simply the best') hurriedly yielded to the connoisseur. I had already, so I said, perceived a dozen or more things to marvel at: not least, our hero's equable response to his tormentors. What a guy. And there had been one or two subtle flick-ons to be relished, the odd imaginative scurry into space, a couple of instant lay-offs under pressure. 'Did you see *that*?' I'd nudge my friend.

But he'd seen nothing much. And by the end, his smile was more patient than benign. 'Well sure,' he said, 'you can tell that he's got class.'

You couldn't, actually, unless you'd been at the Lane last week, when Greaves got four. 'The thing is,' I said, 'they wouldn't *let* him play.'

Would Paul Gascoigne ever inspire devotion of this order? During that 1986–87 season, I followed his progress as closely as I could from where I was. I watched Newcastle whenever they cropped up on television, which wasn't often, and I checked press reports of their games. Gascoigne, it transpired, was already a North-East celebrity. Born in Gateshead in 1967, he starred in local boys' teams and at fifteen had had a trial for Ipswich – where, ominously, he had been turned down by Bobby Robson. He signed apprentice forms for Newcastle a year later, after leaving school – where he had picked up two CSEs (Grade 4) in English and Environmental Studies – and broke into the first team in August '85. Throughout that first season, he was in and out of the Newcastle side – dropped or injured – and it was not until 1986–87 that he began to make his mark. By the time I 'spotted' him, he had already had one or two run-outs with the England Under-21s and was in line for the Young Player of the Year award. Professional commentators, I learned, had been on to him from the beginning, and other clubs knew him to be Newcastle's danger-man. *Vide* that famous photograph of Vinnie Jones grabbing Gascoigne's 'personal bits and bobs' (as Gascoigne later described them): that was in February 1988. So much for my scouting expertise.

In fact, by 1988 – within a year of my first sighting – Gascoigne was pencilled in as a candidate for England's 1990 World Cup squad. He was also giving the management some headaches – the sort of headaches England managers in particular seem prone to. Publicly Bobby Robson called him 'a little gem'. Privately, we now know, he was troubled by almost everything he heard about Gascoigne's 'character' and 'temperament'. In other words, it was looking like the usual story: the Hoddle story, the Greaves story – individual brilliance versus integrated team play, erratic flair versus dependable work-rate. Alf Ramsey, coach of England's World-Cup-winning team in '66, is said to have originated this managerial suspicion of flair players and bequeathed it to Don Revie, Ron Greenwood and then Bobby Robson. But it was there before Ramsey came along: Len Shackleton, also a Geordie and a joker, had been largely ignored by Walter Winterbottom in the 1950s. Shackleton's clownish ways were now regularly being compared to those of Gascoigne.

And with Gascoigne, it seemed, there would also be a dash of the George Best story, the Stan Bowles-Alan Hudson story – a precocious talent self-destroyed. Rumours from Newcastle spoke of drinking sprees and motoring offences, of mischief and subversion. Dave Sexton, the manager of the England Under-21 team, was renowned as one of soccer's 'deep thinkers'. In his spare time, he read Teilhard de Chardin and, when photographed, looked pensive and austere. Players were said to be in awe of him because they could never understand anything he said. Sexton picked Gascoigne for the Under-21s, then dropped him, then picked him again. The deep thinker could not make up his mind. He could see the talent but he hated the irreverence. At team talks, when Sexton unveiled his complex strategies, Gascoigne would be cracking jokes or pulling faces, or he would go off into a corner and ball-juggle.

The boy could not sit still, could not keep quiet. When told off, he would be contrite, but the itch was plain to see: none of this talk really mattered. And when he took to the field, he played not for the team-plan but for himself, or so it seemed. Sometimes, according to Sexton, he was like a 'chicken with no head', running in all directions, needlessly frantic and aggressive. He hogged the ball, held on to it too long and frequently lost possession in his own half of the field.

But then of course he might do something wonderful – like beat three men, curl a free kick round the wall, split the defence with an outrageously angled pass. At such moments he was indeed a little gem. In spite of his lack of thoughtful preparation, Gascoigne scored twice against Yugoslavia's Under-21s and once against both Portugal and Russia. And he did plenty more besides. There were suggestions in the press that he was ready for promotion. In spite of Sexton's – and his own – misgivings, Bobby Robson 'knew, in my heart, that we could not possibly leave him out of the squad for the World Cup finals in Italy. We would have to cater for him.' He may have known it in his heart, but he did not say it at the time. Gascoigne performed under a large question mark, and it is perhaps to his credit that he never seemed to notice it was there.

A recurrent managerial gripe was to do with Gascoigne's weight. As a child he was small for his age and noticeably fat. Scouts who came to view him usually gave him the thumbs-down at first sight. Robson's Ipswich rejection had more to do with the boy's shape than with his skill. And when Gascoigne joined Newcastle, the team trainer Colin Suggett almost gave up on him because of his compulsive eating. Suggett bullied and scolded and imposed every kind of punishing work schedule but he could not compete with the McDonald's and Mars bars. Gascoigne lost weight in the morning and put it on again by nightfall.

On Jack Charlton's arrival as manager of Newcastle in 1984, Suggett was asked to provide an assessment of the club's playing resources. According to one chronicler, Suggett recommended to Charlton that Gascoigne – 'a disruptive influence' – should be 'released'. Gascoigne was summoned to Charlton's office: to get the sack, it was assumed. After about half an hour, Charlton's door opened, and out came not Gascoigne but Big Jack, with tears running down his face, declaring, 'What a life that boy has had.' An early Gascoigne-watcher reckons that the soft-hearted Jack may have been conned: 'I don't know exactly what Gazza said, but he needed only to talk about his dad running off with someone else, and his mum being left on her own at home, and Jack would have been moved.' A diet was decreed, and the player was given two weeks 'to lose a stone – or leave'. He lost a stone – for the time being. And Charlton later mused: 'I've made some bad mistakes, but getting rid of Gazza would have been the worst.'

In most stories about Gascoigne's early years there are two kinds of authority-figure. There are the big-stick men like Colin Suggett, the drill sergeants. These bring out the delinquent in Gascoigne: nose-thumbing behind teacher's back, getting the lads to laugh at Sir's expense. And then there are the father-figures, shrewd, tolerant and humorous, ready to give talent room in which to breathe, to fool around, but stern and headmasterly when pushed too far. Gascoigne's own father had indeed left home and was something of an invalid: he had a brain haemorrhage in his mid-forties and since then had been unemployable – not quite the rock on which a son might lean. Despite his prankish instincts, Gascoigne did seem to need a senior, a guiding hand, and at Newcastle he was probably fortunate: Joe Harvey, Jack Charlton, Arthur Cox. Each appears to have acknowledged that the youngster needed to be 'catered for', that – perky as he was – he functioned on a worryingly short fuse.

Grinning and fidgeting, desperate for centre stage, this mischief-maker could easily be wounded, made to squirm. In Robin McGibbon's book, *Gazza*, there is an interesting account of the player's half-time response to Vinnie Jones's harassment of him during the 1988 Wimbledon encounter. Jones, in the celebrated photograph, is close-cropped, mean-mouthed, darkly gratified: he's not just grabbing, he's twisting. Gascoigne, cherubic, mop-haired, yelps in agony – who wouldn't? Jones, it transpired, had been detailed to nullify Newcastle's star, to 'give him a rude awakening'. 'Who does he think he is? He thought the whole day was about him and no one else. There were ninety minutes to be played and he was prancing about like he was man of the match already.' Thus Jones has recalled the pre-match warm-up. When the game started, he took to his task with relish. Throughout the first half, he followed Gascoigne everywhere, breathing down his neck, taunting him, threatening him, even spitting in his face. 'Stay where you are, Fat Boy, I'll be back,' he'd say when he had to go off to take a throw-in. And back he would come, slit-eyed and leering, the caricature tough.

And, sad to say, it worked. The Newcastle coach, John Pickering, remembers that after forty-five minutes, Gascoigne was 'in total shock. His eyes were red from rubbing away the tears . . .   Not one of us in the dressing-room had seen anyone treated so badly on a football pitch. Paul didn't say one word and he didn't even swear and shout about what had gone on – just sat in the dressing-room, staring into space.' Gascoigne himself has denied that the Jones experience seriously hurt him, but Pickering's account rings true. 'It moved him deeply,' he says. 'We lost him for a bit.' What, then, did this portend? Did Gascoigne's mischievous star turn require the good-humoured compliance of his victims – at least to the extent of playing by the rules? For the likes of Vinnie Jones, playing by the rules usually meant losing. And there were plenty more defenders where he came from.

It was not Jones's muscle that did the damage that day; it was the incessant nastiness, the sense he gave of despising the clown's party tricks. Gascoigne, still a football innocent, a lad who loved to play, to take the piss, had – so Pickering believed – been 'psyched' out of the game. When it came to a straight contest for the ball, Gascoigne was no softie. In the six months or so since I'd first seen him, he had somehow got leaner and bigger. His upper body was more muscular: he was beginning to get the burly, barrel-chested look of a Maradona or a Dave Mackay. Now *that* would be something for Vinnie Jones to ponder: a twinkletoes who packed a punch, a hard man who could dance.

Two weeks before the clash with Jones, Newcastle played Spurs at St James's Park. Spurs had to win, of course, but many of their fans also wanted Gascoigne to play well – or well enough for Spurs to want to buy him. Hoddle had gone by then, and there was a lot of press talk about Newcastle being ready to sell Gascoigne: to Manchester United, to Liverpool, even – unthinkably – to Wimbledon. Terry Venables, the Spurs manager, had not seen Gascoigne play. This, then, would be the crunch. Irving Scholar, the Spurs chairman, has described what happened:

> At one moment in the first half Gascoigne collected the ball just on the arc of the centre circle in his own half and strode forward. Fenwick went in very forcibly to try and dispossess him, but Gascoigne with just a shrug of his hips shook him off, and Fenwick literally bounced off him . . . Terry and I looked round at each other. We didn't need to say anything, our eyes did the talking. Terry was astonished at the sheer power and strength of a player who was still only twenty, and I am convinced that at that moment Terry decided that Gascoigne was the signing that we both felt the club badly needed.

Paul Gascoigne was transferred to Tottenham in May 1988 for two million pounds – a British record. I didn't know it then and, in my delight at what seemed a correct, inevitable marriage, I doubt very much that I'd have cared, but Gascoigne dithered for some days before signing. It was not that he hated to leave Newcastle. He had been on the lookout for a transfer for some time: Newcastle, he believed, had exploited him from the beginning – at one stage paying him a miserly eighty-five pounds a week. And

Newcastle did not want him to go: in February 1988, they offered him a new contract, worth £1,500 a week, rather more than they could actually afford. He turned it down.

Gascoigne's then-agent, Alistair Garvie, got the impression, he said, that Gascoigne 'wanted away from the environment in which he was living'. In newspaper columns – he was already contracted to the *Sun* – the player spoke poignantly of his roots, his evenings with his real mates down at the Dunston Excelsior Working Men's Club, his rapport with the Geordie fans. In truth, though, the Geordie fans were another reason for him wanting to move on. He had never, he knew, entirely won them over. When he played less than brilliantly, they barracked him. When he played well, they reacted with suspicion: who was he trying to impress? He could never be sure of their esteem, and for Gascoigne this mattered quite a lot. It also puzzled him, and footballers are no good at being puzzled.

And he was always being told that he should leave – by other players, like Chris Waddle, a former Newcastle colleague who had gone to Spurs, and who now had for Gascoigne something of the status of an older brother; by the high-earners he ran into on his Under-21 trips; by the newspapers that traffic in fanciful transfer-talk; by the hangers-on who had spotted his market potential. By the time of the Spurs deal, Garvie – a one-time secretary of Newcastle United – had started to feel out of his depth. The Gazza-deals he had lined up in the North-East had brought him more trouble than profit – largely because Gazza, he reckoned, had become increasingly prickly and grasping. He called in a solicitor, Mel Stein, who was London-based but had Newcastle connections, and an accountant, Len

Lazarus, to help with the fine print. By the time the transfer was completed, Stein and Lazarus had replaced him as Gascoigne's principal 'advisers'.

Why did Paul dither, then? Spurs fans more purist than I might well have been appalled to learn that Gascoigne's first choice was not Tottenham but Liverpool. Liverpool had shown an interest but wanted to hold off for a year. Gascoigne was not prepared to wait but, when approached by Spurs, he asked for a clause in his contract allowing him to leave 'if Liverpool come in at a later time'. Irving Scholar baulked at this: 'I didn't intend us to be a safe parking place for Liverpool.' Mel Stein persuaded Gascoigne to back down:

> Eventually they both returned to the room. Paul Gascoigne said: 'Mr Scholar, I have changed my mind about the conditions I was insisting upon the other day. I don't want any conditions in there concerning Liverpool. I'm a Tottenham Hotspur player and I promise you I will give you everything I have to repay your confidence in me.' He put out his hand and we shook.

This is the way everybody talks in soccer memoirs. In real life Gascoigne rarely uses the first person singular. He says 'us' when he means 'me'. And this Geordie trick of speech may have caused Scholar a few apprehensive moments during the contractual debate. When Gascoigne came down to London for the transfer talks, he insisted on bringing with him a small platoon of his best mates from Gateshead. The lads, he said, were to be housed with him in his posh

Hadley Wood hotel. At around two a.m. on the morning after the contract had been signed, Scholar got a call from the hotel: could anything be done to restrain Mr Gascoigne and his colleagues? They were at that moment roaming the corridors, squirting each other with fire-extinguisher foam and engaging in loud Geordie banter. One of them, Five-Bellies Gardner, had been swimming in the hotel's minia-ture boating lake – a little noisily, they said. The following day, Scholar summoned the lads to his office for a dressing-down:

> But his friends completely disarmed me . . . They were lined up like naughty schoolboys waiting for the head-master to chastise them. Before I could say anything one of them, with a bowed head, looked up and said: 'Mr Scholar, I want to thank you for the best three days we've ever had in our lives.' With such an apology, how could anyone get annoyed with them?

Tottenham

G ASCOIGNE'S MOVE TO Tottenham had made him rich. Not rich like Irving Scholar or Terry Venables, perhaps, but rich enough – for him, for now and for the lads back home in Dunston. Gascoigne had grown up in poverty. Even in Gateshead terms, his family was perceived to be hard-up: four children, father out of work, mother having to do part-time menial jobs. 'Make me a millionaire,' Gascoigne told Garvie when the agent first approached him. The Tottenham deal had not quite done that but it had set him on the road. The signing-on fee was said to be £200,000, the salary around £125,000 a year. In addition there were perks: a house, a car and fat bonuses for good results. Manchester United had been ready to give Gascoigne £5,000 each time he played for England, an offer Spurs no doubt had to top.

'Yeah, that's right, I'm going,' he said, in response to Newcastle fans who called him money-mad, accusations stoked by Newcastle's manager, Willie McFaul, who had offered Gascoigne the earth and been rebuffed, and by those of his former colleagues who could not resist the tabloid coin. 'I'm going to a better club, to make more money.' McFaul suggested that Fattie Gascoigne was riding for a southern fall, and the Newcastle chairman, Stan Seymour, called him 'George Best without the brains.' It was an acrimonious parting, and Gascoigne would later be hauled up before the Football Association for verbal retaliation: he ventured to call Seymour 'clueless' for having sold him to Spurs when his old contract still had a year to run. Gascoigne could scarcely be blamed for now and then losing his rag. When he said he 'belonged' in the North-East, he meant it. He found it hard to accept that the Geordie fans, who'd failed to love him, now saw him as a traitor. He too had been a Geordie fan. He had spent his boyhood dreaming about playing for the Magpies.

I couldn't believe the fixture list when I first saw it: Spurs' first game of the 1988–89 season was against Newcastle at St James's Park. When Gascoigne ran on to the field, the crowd bombarded him with frozen Mars bars: they were on sale outside the ground. Throughout the game they booed and chanted whenever he went near the ball: 'Fattie', 'Judas', 'Yuppie'. In those days it was commonplace for visiting London fans to mock the down-at-heel home crowd with lewd songs about unemployment. From the safety of the away-fans' enclosure they waved thick wads of cash and sent up rhythmic chants: 'Loadsamoney, Loadsamoney.' For the Tynesiders, to have Gascoigne owned by such as these was difficult to bear. What was wrong, they wondered, with the loadsamoney that Newcastle had offered him to stay? At St James's Park that day there seemed to be real hatred in the air. And, as with Vinnie Jones, Gascoigne caved in. He was taken off fifteen minutes before the end, booed all the way. Afterwards, he had to be smuggled out of the back door of his old club.

Throughout his first season at Tottenham, Gascoigne – by his own account – spent almost as much time on the motorway as he did in the deluxe quarters Spurs provided: a hotel first and then a house in Hertfordshire. 'The worst time,' he said, 'was whenever I picked up an injury. I would travel to the North-East after watching our game, but at five a.m. on the Sunday I would have to get up and rush down to White Hart Lane for treatment. As soon as that was finished I would climb into my car and head to the North-East again. On Monday it was a case of clambering out of bed at five a.m. and hurtling down to London. I know it was sheer lunacy, but just a few hours with my family and friends kept me from blowing my mind.'

When he went back to Dunston he had to be careful where he parked his black Mercedes and he kept his portable telephone well out of sight. On the other hand, he wanted to show these new toys to his friends. Surely the Mercedes alone – '190 2.6 complete with rear spoiler, low racing skirt and one-way reflective windows' – was proof enough that he'd been right to leave? He wanted the Excelsior to have a piece of his good fortune. Gascoigne may have been money-mad, but all reports of him agree that, when it came to his 'real mates', he was invariably ready with the readies – over-anxiously so, some reckoned. Certainly his Spurs paymasters might have wished that he could rid himself of one or two of his old ties.

Why should he, though? In the South, he was regarded with amusement as a Geordie hick. Irving Scholar, on first viewing him, observed that he 'was dressed in a slightly old-fashioned way, looking very much like a country boy on his first visit to the Smoke'. And then there were his country habits. At Newcastle, he used to chat up the middle-aged ladies who worked in the ticket office. They were, he said, his 'mums'. 'Do you fancy it?' he would ask Maureen, putting his hand up her skirt. And the mums would laugh it off. 'He'd drive you crackers but you couldn't help liking him – he was stupid, but not in a horrible way.'

At Spurs he tried a similar line with Scholar's assistant, a Ms Masterson, and she recoiled with distaste. 'He's going to be trouble,' she opined. His clothes, his dialect, his manners were all there to be mocked. But then he liked to raise a laugh. He was not easily embarrassed.

And there was the continuing problem of his weight. Later on Terry Venables would recall that when Gascoigne arrived at Spurs there was a section of the crowd that decided to target him – as Waddle, now a god, had once been targeted. 'They said he was miles overweight and too slow. It was a struggle for him at the start. But we couldn't force the weight off him for fear of weakening him.' Gascoigne's 'official weight' was eleven stone seven pounds, but, as he confessed, 'I can put on half a stone in a week. Then I've got to shift it in a week. I've learned to watch it though I admit I still let myself go on Sundays. Then I eat a lot because I know I'll be in next day to work it all off.' 'Eat a lot' we can take also to mean 'drink a lot'. For Gascoigne, the close season – June to August – amounted to three months of Sundays. When a new season kicked off he invariably looked out of shape.

As Britain's most expensive footballer, Gascoigne was also the target of the tabloids. For them the script was already written: simple Northern lad gets dazzled by bright lights. Before the new season with Tottenham had begun, at least three Gazza scandals were revealed. The 'night-club bust-up' story was followed swiftly by the 'high jinks on pre-season Swedish tour' story. Then came the 'former model tells all' tale: 'Gazza persuaded me to drive 180 miles to have sex with him.' Gascoigne was new to this game. His advisers wanted him to court publicity, to put his name to ghosted columns, to dress up for photo-shoots, to foster the lovable 'clown prince of soccer' image. He may even have believed that he had some good mates down Fleet Street way. Why then these lies, if lies they were? Why this intrusiveness, this dirt?

In his first year at Tottenham, Gascoigne did just enough to neutralize the terrace malcontents, without quite winning hearts and minds. At Tottenham, hearts and minds enjoy not being won, and it was lucky for him that his arrival coincided with the signing of Paul Stewart. Stewart was expensive too – more than one million pounds from Manchester City – and he was good-looking in a beach-boy way, and vain. Also, he seemed to be no good; that is to say, *really* no good, not just a little slow to find his form. He was soon soaking up the derision that might have been Gascoigne's.

A cheeky goal against Arsenal in September earned Gascoigne a truce and, when he settled, he served up sufficient moments of high skill to compensate for his emerging tendency to disappear from games he could not dominate. Most of these moments came from dead-ball strikes – spectacular free kicks from thirty yards, Brazilian-style. Against Notts County, Derby, QPR, he bent the ball so craftily into the top corner that the goalies could only stand and stare. Against Derby, the victim was Peter Shilton; against Rangers, David Seaman. To the fans, these details mattered. Shilton and Seaman put on airs. There were also several glorious near-misses, a fair supply of tricky solo runs and some incisive interplay with Waddle. Next year, it was believed, these two would click.

The season was crowned with a goal, against Luton, that sent the fans off happy for the summer break. Gascoigne got the ball deep inside his own half and moved forward, head high, chest out, arms spread, as if to say: 'Come on, then, take it off me if you can.' Then he accelerated and by the time Luton reacted he had reached the edge of their area, with only two men between him and the goal, one to his right, one to his left. The two hesitated as he ran towards them: should they close down the middle path or hold ground in case he swerved? He came at them dead straight, and gaining speed. They pounced, but they were half a second late. Instead of pincering the invader, they smacked into one another, face to face. He'd glided through the gap. The two sat there, marvelling, as Gascoigne stepped round the keeper and, with a delighted flourish, scored. For an English league game, this was an unusual goal. And yet it was also about as simple, as uninstructed, as a goal could be, a playtime joy.

Gascoigne's second year at Spurs, 1989–90, was the run-up to the World Cup finals in Italy, and every league game he played was treated as an argument for or against his inclusion in the England side. It was indeed the Hoddle saga all over again. In the months leading up to the 1982

Spain finals, the debate over Hoddle had been relentless and exasperating: one ineffectual game and he was written off. Could this brilliant but inconsistent player be fitted into a team plan? With Hoddle the fear was that he was too meek, too disinclined to put the boot in. With Gascoigne it was suspected that the boot might go in all too eagerly, that he would be the one to pick the fights.

In a game against Crystal Palace in November 1989, Gascoigne was booked for a foul and then argued with the referee. The *People* commented: 'If Gascoigne should produce this sort of over-the-top reaction in the steamy killing fields of the World Cup, God help him. And us!' And this was typical of his press coverage during the first weeks of the season. David Lacey of the *Guardian* complained that this novice lacked technique: 'Add to this an endless flow of backchat to officials and opponents and it is possible to believe that he still has some way to go before he reaches the stature as a player that he clearly is as a marketable media persona.' Gascoigne, said Lacey, was 'like the farmer's boy who discovered roast pork by burning down the pigsty. It is necessary to judge the end product against the amount of damage that may have been done along the way.' Patrick Barclay of the *Independent* sneered at Gascoigne's 'comic-book dribbling'.

And Gascoigne, impressively oblivious to such analyses, seemed intent on undermining his own cause. In 1989–90, he was booked ten times, often for 'dissent' but sometimes for taking a wild kick at an opponent. He broke his arm elbowing a Coventry defender in the face and was sidelined for a month. He threw a punch at Chelsea's John Bumstead, with Bobby Robson sitting in the stand.

'What can you do?' said Robson, after the Bumstead incident. And throughout the year he wavered publicly. He picked Gascoigne a few times as a substitute – ten minutes against Saudi Arabia, five against Denmark – but found it hard to take the ninety-minute plunge. He seemed to fear that by doing so he would be giving the wrong signals – to the player, to the press. At times he gave the impression that he merely wanted to be seen as a man who did not take decisions lightly. Certainly, on the subject of Gascoigne, he liked to think aloud. Against Albania, with England three up, Gascoigne was sent on for the final twenty minutes. He made one goal and scored another. Afterwards, Robson denounced him to the press for having disobeyed instructions: 'We needed two balls out there. One for Gascoigne, and one for the others.' His final verdict was: 'Daft as a brush.'

According to a team-mate, Gascoigne was 'hurt and angry'. Robson's crack had made him 'want to prove, more than ever, what he could really do'. But at England's next training session, he turned up with a brush shoved down his sock, and to Robson, the jest was further evidence that 'it was all just a bit of a laugh to him, really'. The boy was, well, just a boy. 'He's got to learn about the game, how to play it properly – he's still like a kid playing backstreet football. Lot of talent, lot of freshness, there's unbelievable things he'll do – but I'm talking about playing Argentina or Brazil, about being in the last eight in the world. You have to be utterly reliable.' Like Sexton, Robson could not take seriously a player who seemed not to take *him* seriously. At strategy talks, Gascoigne 'would listen to what I was saying and come back with "Oh, aye, all right. OK, I know," ' but

Robson could see that his wisdom was going 'in one ear and out the other'.

If Gascoigne really was wounded by Robson's brush joke, he was not slow to turn the wound to profit. A joke-book called *Daft as a Brush* came out in November 1989, and there was talk of Gascoigne facing a charge from the Football Association of 'bringing the game into disrepute': the book carried a few swear-words and was rude about referees. Gascoigne swiftly 'disassociated himself' from the publication, and – according to Venables – was 'very upset' that he had been made to seem rough-tongued. The *Guardian* was not convinced: 'Reports that the player was in tears over the affair must be taken on trust, since the only previous recorded instance of Gascoigne's lachrymal ducts being tested was when the hand of one Vinnie Jones grabbed a tender part of his anatomy. Whatever the rights and wrongs of the present controversy, it is surely time for Gascoigne, and those who advise him, to decide if he is going to become an international footballer who is a bit of a character or a character who might have been an international footballer.'

This was snootily put – again by David Lacey – but there was truth in the suggestion that Gascoigne's handlers were butter-fingered, allowing the player to get into 'impish' promo-stunts when they should have been highlighting his 'maturity', his dedication to the cause. On the morning of a 'B' international against Italy, Gascoigne was pictured in one paper with his tongue out and a wild look on his face. The effect was to make him seem oafish and deranged, not at all the sort of man to whom you would entrust a nation's pride. And there were 'interviews' in which Gascoigne whinged about a 'conspiracy' to exclude him from the England team. To the *Sun* he confided that perhaps 'It would be better for everyone concerned if I was playing abroad . . . For a start I wouldn't be able to read the papers – even if I was getting stick.' When he was at Newcastle, he 'had no worries whatsoever. All I did there was think, eat and drink football . . . Everything was so uncomplicated . . . I love the game but I think I'm playing in the wrong era. You see games on telly and someone scores a great goal from twenty yards, but then you get the analysts saying someone was offside and criticising the defenders. It's all negative, when football was meant to entertain. That sort of thing does me in. It's like a cancer slowly killing a healthy body.'

Admittedly, it was not easy for Messrs Stein and Lazarus to package a fake Gascoigne when the real man was always likely to unite the parcel, but for those of us who were desperate to see Gascoigne perform in Italy, every day during the run-up to the World Cup was suspenseful. Would Gascoigne, or one of his allies, push Robson into a corner from which he might not be able to escape?

At the end of the 1989–90 season, Gascoigne put together a string of first-rate performances for Spurs. Against Nottingham Forest and Manchester United, he was at his try-and-stop-me best. He got booked against Forest for arguing with the referee and almost gave away a goal against United with one of his notorious forty-yard back-passes, but in both games he was the dominating figure. And Gary Lineker, playing alongside him, was looking good, not least because of Gascoigne's service. It was probably the United game that did the trick: in a two-one victory for Spurs, Gascoigne made United's Neil Webb and Bryan Robson seem cumbersome, not up to scratch. Neil Webb was ahead of Gascoigne in the England queue and Bryan Robson was, of course, the King. When Gascoigne scored, it was Robson he left standing. And the England manager was there to see it happen – and to see Gascoigne glowing with delight at his own mastery, every so often gesturing to Venables on the Spurs bench, as if to say: '*Now* he can't leave me out.'

A few days later, Gascoigne was in the England team against Czechoslovakia at Wembley. This, everyone agreed, would be the big one, the very last last chance. Before the game, according to Pete Davies in his book *All Played Out*, Gazza was more than usually 'coiled up'. 'In the tunnel beforehand, he nearly decapitated me, bouncing a ball off the wall bare inches from my head, with a really manic aggression.' And team-mate Tony Dorigo has recalled that, 'He was nervous and tense, and sweating up through the stress of it all. I noticed his face getting redder than usual, and his twitches were more evident that day too. I don't know any player who had so much expected of him as Gazza had on that night.'

And in the opening moments of the game, we feared the worst. Gascoigne was diving into tackles, he looked frenzied; he would surely break something or get booked. The referee seemed to be telling him to watch it, but it was not at all clear that he was listening. And then he found relief: a stunningly accurate long pass that sent Steve Bull in for England's first goal. Gascoigne seemed to know then that he'd done it, that now he could relax and simply play. And play he did, as if the field belonged to him, but with subtlety and calm. He even managed to make Bull look deadly. Scored one, made three was Gazza's final tally, and the goal he scored was a beauty, a last-minute solo flourish.

It was by far the best game he had played for England, and this time there could be no talk of errant individualism, of not playing for the team. It was he who had made the team look like a team. There had been a few of his old tricks, but on the whole it was his imaginative distribution that had most impressed. Afterwards, Jozef Venglos, the Czech manager, seemed baffled: 'Gascoigne does not look like an English footballer,' he said.

'Maybe it's the old French blood in me coming out,' was Gazza's explanation. 'It's when I start eating the snails and garlic that I'll get worried.' He said this a year later. On the night he was less affable. As the hero left the field, a television crew approached him for a quote. He brushed them off: 'I hate the press.' And yet that same morning he had appeared in a circus clown's rigout on the back page of the *Daily Mirror*. 'The cameramen,' says Davies, 'tapped their heads and turned away.' And Bobby Robson? At the press conference he was invited to admit that Gascoigne had finally arrived. He said: 'All right, tonight he's passed the test. He's slimmer, fitter, he's matured, far better discipline. But you're still not a player after one match.' To Don Howe, his assistant, he said much the same – or says he said: 'Right, we'll have to see if he can do it again. We won't leave him out – we'll pick him again against different opposition and see if he can do it again.'

So, we could breathe again. We could even start looking forward to the summer. And it probably did wonders for Gascoigne's relationship with Robson that on the morning when the England squad assembled for the flight to the World Cup, the pair of them were in the news. ROBSON FINALLY ADMITS: I'M QUITTING, was one headline. Beneath it, in much larger, blacker type was GASCOIGNE WINE BAR PUNCH UP. Robson would be leaving his job after the World Cup – he would become manager of PSV Eindhoven in the Netherlands – and although the Football Association were denying that he had been sacked, they were not trying to make him change his mind.

The Gascoigne story was one that we seemed to have read before: Gazza, outside wine bar with girlfriend (twenty-one-year-old Dunston lass Gail Pringle) is approached by thirty-one-year-old out-of-work non-drinker Anthony Marshall. Marshall says something and Gazza proceeds to black his eye, break his nose and chip several of his front teeth – all by himself. 'I was also dragged along the pavement,' said Marshall, 'badly scourging my left shoulder.' Gascoigne had been questioned by police and then let go. Marshall's mother thought the player should have been locked up.

Arriving at Luton airport, Gascoigne was surrounded by reporters. 'Give it a rest,' he said. 'Why don't you sling it?' Later, according to one of these reporters, 'he had a twenty-minute heart to heart with Robson at a side-table in their hotel restaurant.' Robson, we learned, had greeted Gazza with: 'I hear you've had a day of it as well.' At last the two had bonded: manager and player, wise father-dodgy son, co-victims of the scribblers. Robson made no mention of the wine-bar story; nor, at the time, did Gascoigne. Later on, though, when a team-mate suggested he should sue, he said: 'Nah, I whacked the cunt, didn't I?'

World Cup Hero

THE ANTITHESES HAD been there all along but in July 1990, after Gascoigne's World Cup triumph, they were given a new formulation. His immaturity was now being hymned as 'childlike'; his aggression was 'fire', 'guts', 'determination'; his yob prankishness sprang from a simple need to 'entertain'. If Gascoigne had listened to any of the sermons he'd been given by the press over the years, he would have had good reason now to jeer. What if, as advised, he *had* matured? Would Bobby Robson now be calling him 'a lovely boy, really a lovely boy'?

It was the tears in Turin that pitched Gascoigne from soccer bad-boy to the status of national celebrity. England's semi-final tie against West Germany was seen on television by millions who barely knew the rules of football. They knew enough, though, to grasp that our best player had been made to cry. It did not matter that Gascoigne's grief was first of all for himself: the tears came when he was shown the yellow card, which would have meant being suspended for the final if England reached it. The point was: England lost and they had gone down stirringly, unluckily, with grit. The warrior's tears were felt as patriotic tears, our tears. At the very end of the game, the unchildlike Stuart

31

Pearce was crying too, but no one noticed. By then we were *all* crying, and it was Gazza who had shown the way, who'd been the first to sense how badly this defeat was going to hurt.

I know of at least one Gascoigne fan who was glad that England lost the penalty shoot-out. A World Cup Final without Gazza, he said, would have been unbearable, a joyless second best. As it was, the player's Turin tears achieved symbolic resonance, the stuff of posters, T-shirts, scarves and mugs. Shrouds, maybe. If England had triumphed, had gone on to win the Cup, they would have been just tears. They may even have been read as further evidence of Gascoigne's instability. Who could forget Gary Lineker's gesture to the England bench just after Gazza's booking? He had a finger to his head as if to indicate that Gascoigne had gone mental, that he'd cracked.

In fact he didn't crack – in that game or in any other. For a minute or so after the booking he was out of action: gulping for air, doing his strange neck-jerk thing, but looking blank, as if he had forgotten where he was. And then he conquered it, he rallied and began looking for the ball. It is not often that a soccer match affords such close-ups. And it was perhaps this flash of inner drama, this visible raising of his game, that the *Independent* had in mind when it declared: 'If you believe football is a noble pursuit, Gascoigne, in that moment, was noble.'

'Noble' is not a word that the back pages often have much use for, but on this day it did not seem out of place. And we too had been ennobled. From the split-second against Holland when an explosive pirouette took him through two startled Dutch defenders, Gascoigne had altered our expectations; he had even put a strain on our vocabulary. In that instant we, as fans, moved up a league. At last and maybe just for once we had a player of world class – or rather a player who was not afraid to *be* world class, who could treat the Gullits and Van Bastens, the Baggios and Viallis, as if they were just another mob of big lads in some Gateshead school yard. It was rumoured that during the Dutch game Gazza had made fun of Gullit's dreadlocks and asked Rijkaard how much he was getting from AC Milan. We loved to hear about this kind of thing. We were so used to treating the opposition with respect and to being more than happy when they almost did the same for us. This Gazza was sublimely disrespectful.

We had not reached the World Cup semi-finals since 1966, and, but for Gascoigne, we would not, in 1990, have got beyond the last sixteen. Against the Cameroons it was his heroic surge that won us the penalty that mattered; against both Egypt and Belgium it was one of his pin-point free kicks that saved the day. And altogether he seemed able to raise the team's morale, its 'self-belief'. Clench-fisted, pop-eyed, snarling, he often looked just like a fan. He looked fanatical. On the terraces each week you can see that kind of angry, life-or-death commitment, and it's not a pretty sight. With Gazza, it was translated to the pitch, a grudge come true. The 1990 World Cup has been described as one of the most boring of all time. But not for us. We will remember it as the best since 1970. With '70, apart from Banks's save and that photo of Bobby Moore and Pele swapping shirts, it is names like Astle and Bonetti that stick in the mind – two losers. This 1990 loss, we felt certain, would always be recalled as Gascoigne's victory.

How then to repay him?

When the England team returned from Italy, a grateful nation was more than ready with the spoils. One hundred and twenty thousand fans were at Luton airport for the great home-coming and most of them, it seemed, had turned out to welcome Gascoigne. And although they may not have expected to find their hero laurelled and aloof, eyes modestly downcast, chin resolute, even the most resilient of his admirers were nonplussed by Gazza's coronation garb: a pair of gigantic tie-on plastic boobs plus pendulous beer belly. There he was, atop a roofless bus, the apotheosis of yuk, and grinning wickedly as if he had pulled off some stylish comic coup.

For those soccer aesthetes who had begun to portray him in the subtlest of heroic hues, this was a cruel coming down to earth. We had seen Gazza before dressed as a clown, as a cowboy, even as a sugar-plum fairy, and we had heard more than enough about his over-the-top japes: how he filled Chris Waddle's tea-kettle with shampoo, spiked Bobby Robson's pre-match orange juice, booked sunbed sessions for black team-mates, and so on. We knew about these things and we had learned to live with them, or so we said. Even during the World Cup he had pulled a few clod-hopping stunts. These too we were able to forgive. When, before one match, he stuck his tongue out during the national anthem, this meant he was relaxed, puckishly unfazed. When he threw his drink at Paul Parker because Parker was caught talking to the press, this meant that he was suitably fired-up. All this we could handle. After all, the lads seemed to get a lift from Gazza's pranks. They thought he was nutty, but he made them laugh. And they seemed to like it when he told reporters to fuck off. Well, fair enough. These plastic boobs, though, coming when they did, and on television, just as we were musing most sagaciously upon his merits, his complexities, somehow had the impact of a personal rebuff. One thing was clear: our hero didn't need to be worshipped by the likes of us.

Seen in this way, the boobs rig-out could perhaps be filed under 'personal integrity', read as a sturdy declaration of intent. Gazza would remain unspoiled, or remain spoiled, as some might think. 'I want to be mesel',' he'd often said. We would soon be learning more about that self, more maybe than we wished to know.

At Luton, when the fans dispersed, Gazza was able to slip away into his father's Dormobile and make for Gateshead. He was accompanied by the *Mail on Sunday*, which had paid a fortune for his first exclusive interview since the World Cup. The *Mail on Sunday* was there when Gazza arrived at the door of the Excelsior and said: 'I'm gaggin' for a pint.'

It was very, very emotional, what happened in the club that night. This was England, that special part of it, saying: He is one of ours.

You have seen our Gazza, and now you know what it means to be a Geordie. Now you know about the skill and the wit and the passion and the humour, and, above all, the utter determination – no matter how tough the going gets – not to let anyone roll over them.

35

Hardy wrote about another England in another time and called it The Return of the Native. This was The Return of the Hero – young Paul, born 22 years ago not far from the club in a terraced council house in Pitt Street . . .

Paul has been coming here since he was eight. The bairn in the corner with the Coke and the packet of crisps, while his Dad . . . bought his pints. Ever since then Paul has been part of the heart of the place. He says: 'It's the only place I come in, shut the doors, chalk my name up on the snooker board, and just be me. Just the same as everybody else.'

This was July 1990, and for the next three months Gascoigne was rarely off the front pages of the *Sun, Star, Mirror* and *Today*. The *Sun* had him under contract for £120,000, and this meant that its three rivals had to appoint full-time Gazza-watchers to follow him from *Wogan* to Madame Tussaud's to Downing Street, where he scored a PR bull's-eye by giving Thatcher a big hug: 'She's cuddly, like me.' For the Downing Street visit he sported a mustard-yellow suit with floral beach-shirt – an ensemble that helped to earn him the Menswear Association's award of Britain's Best Dressed Man.

The papers were now full of Gazza's 'estimated earnings'. There were lists of his endorsement contracts: football boots, sportswear, aftershave (his Brut sponsors had to smile when he said, 'It's for pooftahs, isn't it?'). There were catalogues of his memorabilia – from duvet covers to real-tears crying dolls – and breakdowns of his personal appearance fees: two grand for opening a pizza parlour, three grand for a supermarket, a hundred grand for a television commercial. Stein and Lazarus, we learned, were 'fielding' fifty calls a day. They no longer projected Gazza, they protected him. If even half the offers were accepted, the player would have no time in which to play. Lazarus announced: 'We are only proceeding with those deals where we are satisfied with the companies plus the quality and image of the product, to protect Gazza's good character.'

Luckily, Gascoigne's family rallied round; they were prepared to share the load. For £3,000 you could get to photograph his mother; for £1,000 she would give you an interview – about herself. For speaking of her son she charged extra. His sister Anne-Marie was more expensive. Two thousand pounds to talk about her acting career; £2,000 for a photograph. For Paul-talk much, much more. Gascoigne's own price was £10,000 per interview.

Now and again Gazza was prepared to talk for free. In October, he released a pop record, a version of Lindisfarne's 'Fog on the Tyne' (on the B-side you got 'Geordie Boy', with lyrics by Lazarus and Stein). For the record launch, Gascoigne agreed to 'meet the press'. An inspired interviewer from *Time Out* turned up bearing gifts—a battery-operated seal that did football tricks and an inflatable guitar – and as a result got something of a scoop: a Gazza interview that was not entirely grudging and defensive. The presents went down well; they broke the ice. 'Cheers mate. Brilliant. Thanks very much.' In gratitude, Gazza tried hard to say something about his musical tastes: 'Phil Collins, I think every one of his is fantastic. Billy Ocean. I dunno. I just like a good song. I'm not really a big music man.' The 'Fog on the Tyne' recording was, he said, an attempt to emulate

Glenn Hoddle and Chris Waddle, who in the eighties had had a hit with 'Diamond Lights'. 'They done it so I thought it would be good to follow them. Theirs did well – didn't it? – got to number eleven.' He then started strumming his rubber guitar. 'I'll keep this, use it on me next video. I bet you I do. I wish I'd had it beforehand, it would have been great on the video.'

So far, so good. When *Time Out* switched to soccer, Gascoigne 'visibly relaxed'. But then he was asked about the press:

> The English press treat football like a joke. All they do is look for bad bits; every week, bad bits. You never see the good side of it. They've been writing great about me but people should realise that I had nearly two years of shit off them, you know. Nearly two years of absolute crap, slaughtered by them.
>
> With myself they've been really good. But the news people, the news guys, have been right bastards. I'd love to see some of them come into the local pub I go to in Newcastle and see how brave they are then. They're all soft; all they can do is write the front page of the newspaper and give somebody stick. They're cowards.
>
> Girls I wasn't seeing but they put them in the paper, a girl I was supposed to be having an affair with, which was untrue. Some girls go in the paper and say, I've been with Paul Gascoigne. I mean, it's all right for me, she could be a good-looking girl so the lads are like 'cor!' even though I don't like it. What does this girl feel like? She must feel like a right tart.
>
> They camp out at the end of the drive in cars, like

little kids. I mean those people have got to go back to their families. Imagine one of them going home and his wife saying, 'How did your day go?' 'Great. I sat outside Gascoigne's house all day and all night waiting for him to come out.' His wife must say, 'What do you want to do that for, you prick?'

This at least sounded like something Gascoigne might actually have said. And the sense of grievance was well-founded. The press attitude to Gazzamania was not so much ambivalent as straightforwardly two-faced. He was canonized at the back of the paper and terrorized at the front. In August, at the height of his celebrity, the news guys decided to take over his 'love life', which hitherto had not been much discussed. Since his move to Spurs, Gascoigne had lived in Hertfordshire with Gail Pringle, his girlfriend from Dunston. During the World Cup, Gail went out to join him for the last days of the tournament and was eagerly sized up by the hacks. 'It was all so predictable,' said one, 'the first time any of us saw her, we knew her days were numbered. How long would it be, asked the cynics, before this lovely, unspoiled girl would be replaced by a String-fellows bimbo? The truth is, alas, these days that for any girl who finds the frog turned into a handsome prince, life is unlikely to end happily ever after.'

And so it came to pass. A month after the World Cup, one Heidi Shepherd appeared on the *Sun* front page in suspender-belt, G-string and 'provocatively opened black leather jacket'. Heidi, the *Sun* said, was Gazza's new delight. A few days later, the *Mail on Sunday* signed up Gail Pringle's lachrymose account of 'How I Lost Gazza to the

World'. Things used to be so wonderful, she said. 'When we were together we just rented a video and picked up a bottle of Asti Spumante with a Chinese takeaway. We liked curling up on the couch together.' After the World Cup, everything had changed. 'When he came back from Italy, he was always looking over his shoulder. We were living in a goldfish bowl.' And then came Heidi Shepherd – or rather, then came the *Sun*'s photograph of Heidi Shepherd. 'When the papers had a story about Paul and another woman he would always deny it and tell me not to believe what I read. But now I don't know what to believe.'

The truth seems to have been that Gascoigne had indeed wanted to move on, that Heidi Shepherd – a Dunston neighbour – was largely a *Sun* fantasy, and that it was Gail who made the break, telling the supportive *Mail on Sunday*: 'The truth is that if he had been a postman or something we would have been happy forever.' But for Gazza there would soon be other Heidis. In October, blonde dental assistant Natalie Barnes admitted to the *Star* that she was 'the new lady in his life'. The *Star* sent one of its girl-sleuths to confront the 'Romeo soccer star' with these new allegations. 'We thought the fun-loving superstar would be delighted to chat about his sexy new pal . . . but fiery Gazza seemed to think we were stirring things up. When I walked up the path of his luxury home, he rushed out with a huge pan of minestrone soup and tipped it all over me.' Meanwhile, Natalie was already lamenting the end of the affair. On her birthday, she said, Gazza had done her wrong, choosing to go off 'for a riotous West End night out while she sobbed broken-hearted over his absence'.

These Gazza romances were identically structured: simple,

home-loving, marriage-seeking lovely gives all to beer-swilling sexual opportunist. What Gascoigne liked above all, the papers said, was bevvying with his coarse-grained Gateshead cronies, but with the occasional element of 'Cor!' The bet was that *Star* and *Sun* readers, male and female, would instantly recognize the type – as, no doubt, they did. And so presumably did Gascoigne, but the coverage still seemed to get him down. He appeared at times to be genuinely baffled by the motivation: was he loved, or wasn't he? Why the destructiveness, the wish to wound? After Tottenham's first game of the new season, he declared: 'I'm fed up with all this girl-talk. I have split up with Gail but I don't want to have another girlfriend. It took me twenty-five minutes to get going playing football because of all this hype about a new girlfriend. It seems the only place I am safe these days is out there on the football pitch.'

'He's a very sensitive boy,' Tottenham coach Terry Venables had said, even before the Turin tears, and during the first months of the new season he had to repeat it more than once. Gascoigne started well, as if relieved to be back where he was 'safe', where he knew what to do and who to be. And he was welcomed. Every ground he played at was packed out, and he knew that the extra fans were there because of him. Post-Italy euphoria was evident, and although cries of 'fat boy' and 'big-head' were heard from some opposition fans, there was an odd suspension of the usual enmities. When Spurs played away, with Gascoigne and Lineker on show, supporters were able to relive those great moments of the summer.

Throughout September, Gascoigne was ablaze: a hat-

trick against Derby, four against Hartlepool in the Rumbelows Cup, a stunner against Manchester City, and, in
between, some breath-taking moments of high skill. For five
weeks, he was unstoppable. Perhaps the will to stop him
was not there. After all, players are fans too and would also
have been glued to the World Cup. By October, though,
things had begun to tighten up, and Gazza found himself
back in the old routine: the shirt-tugging, the sneaky
elbows, the wind-up repartee. Against Aston Villa on 1
October, he was tracked everywhere by Paul Birch, got into
a spitting-fight with him and later took a swing at Paul
McGrath. 'He was pulled back nearly every time he went
past someone,' said Venables, 'and that is frustrating for
supporters. They want to see what happens when he has
gone past them.'

Well, some do. Against QPR a week later there was
another flare-up, and Gascoigne was booked for yelling at
the referee. Venables again sprang to his defence. Was the
manager suggesting that Gascoigne deserved special protection? This notion was swiftly worked up into a 'talking
point', and several papers began dusting down their sermons from the year before. David Miller in *The Times*
intoned: 'Gascoigne needs protection from himself.' His
'immaturity' was still a problem. He thinks he's funny,
Miller said, but his play-acting was in truth 'about as funny
as a puncture.' Stuart Jones, also in *The Times*, seemed to
agree: 'Gascoigne is going to cause some explosions unless
he learns to lengthen his fuse.' There could be no excuse for
his excessive 'petulance'. Mostly the fouls on him were
occasioned by his 'running style': 'With his arms flailing, his
elbows flapping and his hands grasping he resembles a late

commuter attempting in desperation to board a train which is leaving the platform. Anyone in his way risks having the contours of their upper body instantly and painfully rear-ranged.' True enough, perhaps, but wasn't this the same 'determined' style that we'd been drooling over just eight weeks before?

There was an unpleasant hint of backlash, too, in the way the papers resurrected the old Vinnie Jones dispute. After Spurs played Sheffield United – where Vinnie was now lodged – Jones called Gascoigne 'flash', 'a bottler' and (rather oddly) 'not the same lad I knew eighteen months ago'. He predicted that Gascoigne would 'get hurt one day with all that standing on the ball and taking the piss. Whenever I play against him, he disappears. He never came out for the game. He didn't fancy it. I said, "Come on, take me on," but he bottled it.' Gascoigne had indeed been substituted in the second half, after a largely anonymous performance. He had spent most of his time on the pitch making rude gestures to Dave Bassett, the United manager, who – pre-match – had called Gascoigne 'a buffoon'. 'Gascoigne,' said Bassett, 'goes around ruffling hair and making gestures and gets away with it. But if my kids behaved like him they would be given a good smack and sent to their room.'

All this was given headline treatment, but the whole thing somehow seemed contrived. So too did Gascoigne's run-in with George Best. In the papers and on television, Best was being prodded for his verdict on Gascoigne and, when it came, it was brutally dismissive. He was tired, he said, of seeing his own name crop up in pieces about Gazza. Was Gazza as good as Best had been? Would Gazza go the same way – i.e., downhill, and self-propelled? Best's view was that Gascoigne wouldn't last: 'He's not good enough. He's a false idol. He's hailed as a superstar because there aren't any, there's a void. There's more to the making of a superstar than a couple of fair games in an abysmal World Cup. I survived because I was the best. Twenty years ago he would have been an average midfield player.' If Gascoigne had anything, he said, it was a sort of childish ebullience, but this would quickly fade. He gave Gazza two or three seasons at the most. It was sad to hear Best talk this way, with seeming bitterness, but it was sad also to hear Gascoigne, invited to respond, describe his precursor as a 'scum bastard' and a 'drunken fat man'.

In October, England played its first game since the World Cup – a European Nations Cup qualifier against Poland – at Wembley. When the England team ran out, Gascoigne lingered in the dressing-room and then trotted out alone, to a tumultuous welcome. But after the match, England's new manager, Graham Taylor, said that England had been playing with ten men – and it was pretty clear that the missing one, in his view, had been Gascoigne, who had made small impact in a two-nil victory for England. Taylor's comments induced a familiar chill in the hearts of all Gazza-fanciers: were we going to go through all *that* again?

Indeed we were. England's next big game was against the Republic of Ireland – the team we cannot beat, the team that knows how to stamp out midfield artistry. Three days before the match, a piece in *The Times* by Stuart Jones gave us the warning light: 'What should Graham Taylor do with Paul Gascoigne?' – a question that would have been unthinkable three months before.

After Italy, and so soon after Italy, it was infuriating to hear the old worries trundled out: 'Gascoigne runs this way, he runs that. And the ball never comes for Lineker. Gascoigne is off on some private excursion, rousing the terraces but too often not allowing his colleagues to join him on the trip.' This was unfair. If Jones had been at White Hart Lane throughout September, he would have seen Lineker miss at least three chances made for him by Gascoigne. He would also have noticed that three of Gazza's goals came from Lineker 'assists'. The two could play together very well.

But Graham Taylor did drop Gascoigne for the Ireland game. It was not, he said, a Gazza sort of match. The pitch was heavy, and so too were the Irish. To replace him, he brought in Gordon Cowans, a player who had worked under him at Aston Villa: a skilful player but wraith-like, past his best and not in the least suited to the Republic's mud and muscle. Cowans did nothing against Ireland but then nor did anybody else: it was a dreary, watchful draw, one-one. Taylor was neither shamed nor vindicated. Afterwards he said: 'I'm not saying that Gordon Cowans is a better player than Paul Gascoigne. What I am saying is that in this particular game I picked the right side to meet what I knew would happen. It mattered that we kept a clear mind when the onslaught was on.'

A clear mind? Was this a hint? Taylor prides himself on his communication skills, but he also likes to suggest that he knows more than he is saying. He went on:

I would find it very hard to believe that the things that are written about Paul don't affect a boy of twenty-three. Because he is such a gifted footballer, it has to be of concern to me as England manager but it is something I cannot control. It was not a question against the Republic of playing Cowans instead of Gascoigne, it was a question of the team. You can talk about the flaws you may believe are in his character, but I won't. Whatever I think has to be left to me and the player to discuss privately. Throughout my career, when I have had something of a private nature to discuss, it has remained between the player and me.

What did this mean? What was it, of a private nature, that he and Gascoigne needed to discuss? Gazza himself was silent, humbly accepting his demotion, so it seemed. A couple of years later, Taylor would tell us more about this Irish incident. In the meantime, though, we Gazzamanes were left with the feeling that a tide had turned, that something might go wrong, or had gone wrong.

Don't Cry for Gazza

'WHO IS GAZZA?' asked Mr Justice Harman in the High Court in September 1990. The judge was hearing an application from Paul Gascoigne Ltd for an injunction against Penguin Books' impending *Gazza*, an 'unauthorized biography' by Robin McGibbon. The argument for the plaintiff was that the name 'Gazza' had been trademarked and that McGibbon was in breach of copyright.

'Paul Gascoigne is a very well-known footballer,' explained Michael Silverleaf, Gazza's counsel.

'Rugby or Association football?' asked the judge.

And at this Silverleaf seemed to wilt: 'Association football. He plays for Tottenham Hotspur Football Club and played in the World Cup this summer. As a result of his performance he has come to be very greatly recognized by the public in this country.'

The judge still didn't get it. 'Isn't there an operetta called *La Gazza Ladra*?' he inquired. Silverleaf could not say. The judge went on: 'Do you think Mr Gascoigne is more famous than the Duke of Wellington was in 1815?'

'I have to say I think it's possible,' said Silverleaf. For Mr Justice Harman, this revelation was enough to swing the case in Penguin's favour. The Iron Duke, he seemed to recall, had had no 'right of action' against upstart biographers, although he disapproved of them. Silverleaf's plea that 'times have changed' was met with a final, withering riposte: 'But the law fortunately hasn't. . . I cannot see that Mr Gascoigne has at this time any reputation in this class of goods which could be appropriated by the defendants by publication of this work.'

A defeat, then, for Gazza – or rather for Mel Stein and his legal team. Stein's concern in bringing the suit, or so it seemed, was that McGibbon's book would come out before his own ghost-work-in-progress, *Gazza: My Life in Pictures*. Stein's literary plans for Gazza were ambitious: after *My Life in Pictures* there would be *Gazza's Football Year*. Each of these publications would be billed as 'by Paul Gascoigne with Mel Stein' and each would be heavily pictorial – about fifty words a page. Even so, they would maintain an affable control of Gascoigne's image. He would come across in them as a shrewd, modest, quick-witted, easy-going sort of guy, with a workmanlike command of tabloid prose. If there were rough edges, Paul would be seen as fortunate to have a sophisticate like Stein to watch over him. Len Lazarus would also receive a grateful mention in both works.

McGibbon's book, although reverential and somewhat stodgily composed, was in a different bracket, and not at all aimed at the juvenile-fan readership that Stein seemed to be soliciting. In commercial terms, there was no rivalry, and the trademark argument had scant hope of success since Gascoigne had been known publicly as 'Gazza' long before Mel Stein took over his affairs. Was there something else, then, in the book, that brought the case to court? Gascoigne later complained – 'with Mel Stein' – that the book was full of inaccuracies but he offered no examples. He might plausibly have argued that it was too thorough. McGibbon, a former *Sun* journalist, had done some serious leg-work in the North-East. He had amassed several tape-hours of interviews with Gascoigne's early circle: school-friends, team-mates, teachers, coaches. In consequence, his book was rich in data, some of it merely homely or sentimental, some of it intriguing.

Only one disclosure could be thought of as provocative, and was indeed seized on as a scoop. 'Gazza's Tragic Secret' was on the *News of the World* front page shortly before McGibbon's book appeared. The secret was to do with the player's much-discussed 'mentality', his nerves. McGibbon had discovered that when Gazza was twelve he had seen one of his friends knocked over by a car and killed. The shock had left him with a string of nervous ailments. There were nightmares, bouts of insomnia, crying jags and so on – but there had also been a perceptible change in his day-to-day behaviour. Gascoigne developed severe facial twitches, he stammered, he blinked all the time. There was 'a nervous swallow, a clearing of the throat, which came out as a high-pitched squeak . . . some muscular reaction forced the noise out, particularly when he was under pressure.' Later the squeak turned into a bark. According to one of the Newcastle scouts, Gazza 'would get rid of one affliction, then another would start. When the barking stopped I'd say, "You've got rid of the dog, then, Paul." By then, he had developed another nervous habit – a dry cough or something. I don't think he knew he was doing it. Other lads used to take the mickey and mimic him.'

For Gascoigne's more ruminant admirers, this information seemed to invest their hero with new glamour. For the first time, his off-the-field personality had something more to offer than obscenities and ale, something that rendered him susceptible to abstract speculation. We had seen his spasmodic head movements start up at high-pressure moments during the World Cup. We'd seen him twitch and blink, pull faces, gulp. If we'd been close enough, we might have heard him bark. Now we could connect these symptoms to his child psychology, to a trauma that was itself to be admired: after all, it was not little Gazza who had been knocked over by a car; it was his mate.

There was speculation too that Gascoigne might be suffering from a form of Tourette's Syndrome. Victims of this ailment display 'an excess of nervous energy, and a great production of strange motions and notions: tics, jerks, mannerisms, grimaces, noises, curses, involuntary imitations and compulsions of all sorts, with an odd elfin humour, and a tendency to antic and outlandish kinds of play'. They also show 'a capacity for inspired improvisation'. This did sound like our man. It could also be made to sound like an over-eager version of Lear's Fool. An all-licensed Gascoigne might not be too amusing, but there was much literary appeal in the idea that his yob-nonsense and his soccer artistry might be clinically conjoined.

In *The Man Who Mistook his Wife for a Hat*, Oliver Sacks tells the story of Ray, a Tourette's sufferer who had been fired from a dozen jobs because of his condition. His marriage was in trouble, and his friends, although they liked him, could not help but laugh. It was not just the facial tics that had antagonized employers: there were also the problems of his impatience, his pugnacity and his coarse 'chutzpah'. Ray was given to 'involuntary cries of "Fuck!" or "Shit!"' when he became excited. At games, though, he excelled,

> partly in consequence of his abnormal quickness of reflex and reaction, but especially, again, because of 'improvisations', 'very sudden, nervous, *frivolous* shots' (in his own words), which were so unexpected and startling as to be virtually unanswerable.

Sacks cured Ray with drug treatment so that he now enjoys a new 'spaciousness and freedom' in his life. His wife loves him again, and his friends 'value him as a person – and not simply as an accomplished Tourettic clown.' On the other hand, Ray no longer plays sport very often, and if he does he finds that he has lost his special gift:

> he no longer feels 'that urgent killer instinct, the instinct to win, to beat the other man'; he is less competitive, then, and also less playful; and he has lost the impulse, or the knack, of sudden 'frivolous' moves which take everyone by surprise. He has lost his obscenities, his coarse chutzpah, his spunk. He has come to feel, increasingly, that something is missing.

We did not want something of Gascoigne to go missing. And yet, in the light of McGibbon's revelations and Taylor's gnomic remarks after the Ireland game, we were now more than ever inclined to think of his talent as unstable, under threat. The feeling was well captured by Karl Miller in the *London Review of Books*, who saw the World Cup warrior as 'a highly charged spectacle on the field of play: fierce and comic, formidable and vulnerable, urchin-like and waif-like, a strong head and torso with comparatively frail-looking breakable legs, strange-eyed, pink-faced, tense and upright, a priapic monolith in the Mediterranean sun'.

And another don, John Casey, called Gazza 'the weeping, doomed, inarticulate idol of the working classes'. But if doomed, doomed to what? George Best thought that Gascoigne's gift would simply peter out, he would outgrow it; others believed it would be coached out of him by functional team managers like Taylor; some feared that Gascoigne would do the job himself, that he so little understood the nature of his own genius that he would be unable to protect it from the excesses to which his personality was irreversibly inclined. Or should he go to see Professor Sacks?

On New Year's Day 1991, in a televised game against Manchester United, Gascoigne was sent off for swearing at the referee. Afterwards he raised press guffaws by pleading that, yes, he may well have sworn, but he was not swearing *at* the referee – an explanation which Sacks might not have been surprised by.

The Manchester United game we can now see as the final act of Gazzamania's benign phase. He had been worshipped and he had been warned, and there he was, still at it, was the general cry. But for his sending off, Tottenham might have beaten United that day and thus kept up their perky start to the season. As it was, all hope of winning the Championship must now be written off. For Spurs, it might be said, what's new? But 1990–91 was different from other seasons; this year it mattered that Spurs *seemed* to have a chance of doing well. English clubs had only just been re-admitted to European competitions, after having been banned following the deaths at Heysel stadium, and Tottenham badly needed to persuade the Midland Bank that they would be in on the proceeds.

For several months, the club had been keeping the lid on a worsening financial crisis. During the eighties, Tottenham Hotspur plc, under the chairmanship of Irving Scholar, had been leaking money into various low-grade, money-grabbing schemes that had gone wrong. To make a Spurs fan squirm you had only to mention the executive box mania, the flotation, the diversification into 'leisure-industry' pursuits, the Saatchi and Saatchi ad campaign, the computerized ticketing, the 0898 Hotline, the Hummel shirt fiasco. When Spurs sold Chris Waddle to Marseille for four and a half million pounds, supporters large and small whinged in the streets, or on the East Stand scaffolding, and they whinged some more when it was revealed that the Waddle loot was needed to offset the losses of a Spurs-owned ladies fashion-wear concern. What it all added up to by 1991 was a debt of around fifteen million pounds with interest running at three million pounds a year.

In this year of all years, then, Spurs needed to win something. They also needed to sell something – or somebody. To get into Europe they now had to capture either the Rumbelows Cup (from which they would shortly be eliminated) or, better by far, the FA Cup. To do this, they looked to Lineker and Gascoigne, their most saleable assets. The thirty-year-old Lineker would not fetch much more than the one million pounds they had paid for him (by IOU). Gascoigne, however, was – in age terms – not yet at his peak and might be worth, well, anything: press estimates since the World Cup had ranged from five to fifteen million.

In the end, Spurs went for a best-of-both-worlds solution to the problem: Gazza, according to their master-plan, would win the Cup for them and *then* be sold.

Throughout the second half of the season, Gascoigne was kept out of the rough-and-tumble of the League. He had developed a troublesome groin injury which would eventually need surgery. It was decided that this injury would be nursed from Cup-tie to Cup-tie, and an operation was timed for 11 March. On 10 March, Spurs beat Notts County in the sixth round. This meant they would play Arsenal in the semi-final on 14 April. Gazza thus had a month in which to recover from the operation and to get match-fit.

And how Spurs needed him. In each of the earlier rounds, it was his contribution that had got them through. Against Blackpool in round three, his free kick had set up the winning goal, and against Oxford (round four) he ran the game, scoring twice and sending Venables into raptures: 'Over the years you can always compare a current player with somebody from the past, a player always reminds you of somebody. But in the case of Paul Gascoigne, I don't know anyone who has played like him.' Venables ended up by describing a cross between Dave Mackay and Tommy Harmer, with a dash of Maradona for good measure. The Oxford manager did not demur: 'Gascoigne was so sharp it was unbelievable. You can't stop him. We needed twelve men out there . . . [but] he would still have done the things he did.'

DON'T CRY FOR GAZZA

And so it went on. Against Portsmouth (round five) Gascoigne scored two goals, one with his head, and against Notts County (round six), he won the game in the last minute. No one could remember a Cup-run in which so much had turned on the performance of an individual player, round by round, over the full distance. Well, nearly the whole distance. The big one, against Arsenal, was viewed with dread by experienced Spurs fans. The hype was intensive, the match was at Wembley and Arsenal were top of the league: it was the sort of game Spurs *always* lose. And yet they won – thanks largely to a spectacular Gascoigne free kick in the fifth minute. Some sense of what this masterpiece of a goal meant to the Spurs faithful, the triumph, the astonishment, can be gleaned from the writings of one Stuart Mutler, editor of the *Spur*.

When that big bastud of a free-kick left the right peg of Paul Gascoigne on 14 April, 1991, you could have peeled me off the roof of Wembley Stadium. It was a moment that encapsulated all that was . . . that was . . . BOLLOCKS! Words fail me (as usual).

Is Gascoigne going to crap on the Arse? He is y'know. GET IN THERE, YOU F – ER. Boring I know but that's the way it was.

I can't remember what *I* said when Gazza's shot went in but I don't suppose it was much prettier. Even now, among Spurs fans, a mention of 'the free kick against Arsenal' induces a moment of silent, beaming homage. And for decades this is likely to be so. It was for us what Michael Thomas's last-minute, end-of-the-season, championship-winning goal against Liverpool was for Arsenal, except that *they* were on the receiving end of *ours*.

Spurs went on to beat Arsenal three-one, and the calculators were out in the directors' box. Negotiations had already begun for Gascoigne's transfer, and this goal may have added another million to the fee. Since February Spurs had been checking the Italian market. The big clubs, Juventus and Milan, had shown a tentative interest but had not come through with solid offers. The one really enthusiastic response was from Lazio of Rome. Just before the Notts County game they tabled a bid of five million pounds: a three-year contract, a house, a gang of bodyguards and a hefty signing-on fee, probably one million. For both club and player, the offer was seductive. Even so, Spurs stalled: Gazza, they announced publicly, was not for sale. By March the transfer fee had climbed to eight million: there were handshakes but no signatures. Venables and Scholar, in their separate ways, were trying to raise money elsewhere: each of them had staked his job on the promise that Gascoigne would not be sold.

Lazio meanwhile were telling *their* fans that Gazza – this 'poet and peasant of the free kick' – would very soon belong to them. As a result, the club's VIP membership scheme (£5,000 a head) was doing well. On 25 April, a Spurs contingent plus Mel Stein flew out to Rome, and by the twenty-sixth the deal was done – three weeks before the Cup Final against Nottingham Forest. Gascoigne himself had not yet agreed his 'personal terms', and Venables was still pleading with him not to go, saying that signing for Lazio would be like signing for Norwich. On Cup Final day, though, we knew that this would be Gascoigne's last game for Spurs. Gazza indeed had said as much: 'If I said no, Spurs would go to the wall. I could never have that on my conscience.' For the fans, it was all a bit bewildering. They had been told that winning the Cup would mend the club's finances, but now it seemed that Gazza's Cup heroics had been a farewell gift.

Spurs hadn't actually won the Cup yet, but everyone believed they would, and that Gazza would produce some crowning marvel, the icing on a cake which to some of us already looked a little stale. Gascoigne knew what was required of him, and before the game Terry Venables was edgy: 'I do fear for Gazza with all the pressure he's under. The world is watching him. It's too much. He's only human.' Later on, Irving Scholar would accuse Venables of 'turning the key' on his already wound-up star. In the tunnel, as the teams waited to make their entrances, Gascoigne was sweating and twitching; he was breathing like a bull, somebody said.

None of this was evident during the pre-match presentations. Gascoigne kissed the hand of Princess Di instead of shaking it: cocky but not too cocky. As soon as the game started, though, it became clear that he was on the rampage. After five minutes he launched a chest-high kick at Gary Parker, a foul which in some games might have got him a red card. Would that it had. A few minutes later, Gary Charles carried the ball to the edge of the Spurs penalty area and was about to be closed down by van den Hauwe. And then, into our picture, out of nowhere, came Gazza at high speed. He caught Charles with a swiping tackle and the pair of them went down, with Charles on top and Gascoigne's right leg twisting as he fell. A free kick for Forest which Stuart Pearce hoofed into the Spurs net.

Nil-one. Gascoigne was OK, it seemed. He shuffled back to the halfway line, looking shamefaced. At the restart, though, he ran half a dozen paces and then fell. This time he stayed down, and somehow we knew that it was bad: the physio was leaning over him for far too long, too many of his team-mates gathered round. Then came the stretcher. The cameras closed in, but Gascoigne had an arm across his face. Nayim came on as a substitute and a bit later we saw an ambulance parked at the players' entrance. The word was that Gascoigne had broken his right leg.

Famously it was much worse than that. The player had ruptured an anterior cruciate ligament, the ligament that controlled the movement of his knee joint. This was an injury we'd heard about – much feared, it had ruined a number of promising careers: Brain Clough's, for one. Even if Gazza's knee was saved, it would be months before he could play again. Lazio's general manager was at the Wembley game. Would he want Gascoigne now? Would anyone? Mel Stein has recalled: 'It was a nightmare. It was the Jewish sabbath, so I couldn't ride. I walked thirteen miles home from Wembley on the North Circular without knowing what was happening. "Paul's been four times on the phone already, crying," my wife told me when I got in. "Do you think Lazio will still take me?" he kept asking when I got through to him, and I told him, "Of course they will."'

On Sunday, everyone assessed the damage. There was a certain amount of sorrowing for Gazza, but not much:

even the Stuart Mutlers could not get round the fact that Gascoigne had 'brought it on himself'. It was, said Mutler, 'Haywire City. Yeah, '*course* I knew he was capable of such acts of stupidity. But it was freaking me out to the point of total insanity. I still wanted to love him! But for the Gaz to plummet from such a towering high . . . ? No. I could no longer defend the man. I had to expel him from my soul. Paul Gascoigne. You are a Bastard. Get Out of my Life.' And the *Mail on Sunday* more or less agreed: 'There can be not a scrap of pity for Paul Gascoigne, who entered the game with the mindless fury of a demented child and left, damaged and discredited, upon a stretcher.'

In England the fear that a great talent may have been destroyed was less pressing than the need to pontificate, to gloat. Luckily for Gascoigne, and for the Tottenham finances, the Italians were more generous. 'We consider him still in the family,' said the Lazio president Gianmarco Calleri. 'We've suffered a mortal blow. Gascoigne is a player of whom we have become very fond, a person we like very much, and I, at this point, say that we won't leave Gascoigne on his own.' In Italy, the tackle on Charles was seen as mistimed, badly executed, but not crazy. They saw worse each week in the Italian league – as we did in ours, they might have added. Before leaving London, the Lazio officials visited Gazza in hospital, gave him a £5,000 gold watch and told him to get better soon.

Lazio were somewhat less soft-hearted when it came to dealing with the Spurs money-men. The eight-million-pound offer was reduced to £4.8 million. Lazio would show its good faith by paying out £750,000 immediately and the rest in installments, according to the player's progress. If Gascoigne *was* finished, the money would have to be repaid. For cash-strapped Tottenham, who had feared that the Italians would pull out altogether, a refusal was out of the question. After some dignified dithering they said yes – yes, please. And so far as Gascoigne's own deal was concerned, the original terms would have to be re-thought – although he would very likely still get the million he'd been promised.

Gazza's knee was now world-famous, the object of anxious scrutiny. Sports journalists were deep in *Gray's Anatomy*, discovering for the first time how the limbs they reported on each week actually functioned. John Browett, Gazza's surgeon at London's Princess Grace Hospital, explained to the cameras the full grisliness of the injury and showed, with the help of a plastic model, how he meant to put it right. He would reconstruct the ruptured ligament, he said, by cutting out the middle third of Gascoigne's patella tendon. To each end of this excised tendon he would attach a piece of bone, one piece grafted from Gazza's kneecap, the other from his thigh. He called this his 'little composite'. The composite would then, by keyhole surgery, be threaded into place behind the kneecap and held there with screws and staples. In effect, Gascoigne would be given a new cruciate ligament, stronger perhaps than the original, and would supply the parts himself. The surgeon stretched his little composite like an elastic band, as far as it would go: it didn't snap.

Most people doubted that the hyperactive Gascoigne would be able to endure the grim months of physiotherapy that lay ahead. When in July he was seen on crutches, sticking his tongue out at the cameras, firing his water-pistol at reporters, nobody laughed. Gazza seemed to be limping out of the headlines. There was a brief flare-up later that month when he was arrested outside a Newcastle nightclub for 'alleged assault' – he had fought with two men who were bothering his sister. The incident was chalked up as a black mark: what was the injured player doing outside a nightclub in the first place? Then in September came the story so many seemed to have been waiting for. Another nightclub, another fight, but this time Gazza landed on the floor, and smack on to his wounded knee. The kneecap broke. Five months of treatment appeared to have been thrown away.

DON'T CRY FOR GAZZA was the headline of a long *Sunday Times* investigation into the new knee-break. James Dalrymple was sent to Newcastle to be told by drinkers in the Half Moon in Bigg Market that, on the fateful day, Gascoigne was half-drunk by ten o'clock. 'He was about eight out of ten and rising. But with Gazza it's hard to tell. He looks as if he was born with five pints of a start.' Gazza, Five-Bellies Gardner and a handful of the lads from the Excelsior had begun drinking in Dunston that morning before setting off to watch the Newcastle-Derby game. 'They were just a bunch of lads off to the match on a Saturday afternoon. They weren't looking for no bother. Just a few beers and a laugh.' At the game, Gazza bought himself an 'Haway the Lads' hat, but he and his friends left at half-time 'and spent the next six hours trawling the pubs and wine bars of the city centre.' The trawl ended at Walkers Night Club where, said Gascoigne later on, 'I was on my best behaviour. I signed as many autographs as I could. I was friendly to everyone. Then someone just whacked us, y'know. He just said "Gascoigne" and I thought he wanted an autograph. I dunno why he did it . . . well, I do know – 'cos he's a jealous bastard, that's why.'

The intrepid Dalrymple was in no mood to be conned. His painstaking reconstruction of events did not tally with the account put out by Gazza. Gascoigne claimed that his assailant came at him 'outside the gents' toilet'. But the toilet was directly opposite the bar. Surely someone would have noticed the North-East's biggest celebrity being pummelled to the ground? There was evidence that Gazza was 'unharmed' when he left the club that night. And why was no one pressing for the police to get involved? Gazza's own assault charge was coming up before the beak in three days' time. Could this be of significance?

The *Sunday Times* verdict was that Gazza and his pards pretty much deserved to be assaulted – and on a regular basis, if that could be arranged. They went from club to club, from pub to pub, with their shaved heads, their medallions, their T-shirts, their earrings, their aggressive ribaldry, their Gazza. And Gazza himself was a sort of Comus for the eighties, with his designer gear, his wad of fifties, his Algarve-flush, his photograph-me grin. Said one Dalrymple confidant: 'He moves at the centre of his pack of minders and he tries it on with every girl who crosses his line of sight. He thinks it's all good clean fun – but their boyfriends are Geordie lads just like him, and don't take that sort of thing. The result is trouble wherever he goes. He regards Newcastle as his personal domain.'

The incident is worth dwelling on because it marks the

end of Gazza's 'one-of-the-lads' chapter. He seems to have finally sorted out *why* the just-like-him Geordie boys could so readily turn into jealous bastards. From where they were sitting, broke, on the dole, with dire prospects, there was plenty to be jealous *of* – not least, perhaps, the bright red, hand-made shoes that Gazza wore to Walkers on the night that he got thumped. 'I think the penny's got to drop,' he said. 'I can't go – I'm never going to a nightclub in Newcastle again, you know, never. The thing is I've come to realize that people outside football are not going to give us a chance to be one of the lads. All I want is to be one of the local lads, you know, and they're not giving me a chance. They're jealous. Now I've come to realize that I can't *be* one of the lads.'

When Gascoigne talked like this the press sneered at his 'self-pity'. They'd heard it all before. How could he have imagined that it might be otherwise? Grow up. But in earlier laments, Gazza had been blustering, defiant. This time he sounded genuinely plaintive. People called him 'flash', he said, because he liked to 'stand my mates a drink or two, even if the bill is over the top. It's not me being flash. It's just that I would feel embarrassed in case people would think I was a tight bastard. You can't win. I get on a train and sit in second class and people think, "Tight bastard. Money he's got and he sits in second class." So I think "Fuck them" and go in first class and then they say "Look at that fucking flash bastard in first class." Where do I win?'

And in a *Sun* exclusive he defended the much-maligned Five-Bellies Gardner: 'A tower of strength. He would walk to the end of the world for me. He was crying about the last nightclub incident. He said, "Why couldn't it have been me?" . . . I can't go around not having friends all me life. I've had me friends since I was at Newcastle. I can't say, "Thanks very much. That's it, now I'm a star, sorry lads, you're nothing, now fuck off.""

The broken kneecap set back Gascoigne's recovery by about three months, but in medical terms it was not quite the disaster that it seemed. In spite of having sustained 'a tremendous trauma' the transplanted cruciate ligament was found to be intact. It would have been hard to have devised a sterner test. The surgeon denied that Gascoigne's kneecap broke because it had been weakened by the surgery he'd had. The two injuries, the doctor said, had no bearing on each other. But there must be no further risks. Gascoigne would be 'gated' for eight weeks.

According to all reports, Gascoigne's determination during those eight weeks could not be faulted: he did as he was told, which amounted to several hours of physiotherapy each day, early nights, no social life and not too many laughs. 'Paul's had a fright,' said one of the Spurs physios. 'He's different, still a lovable lad, but he's quietened down a lot. He had to.' He was not that quiet, though. According to John Browett, Gascoigne's 'motivation' was, if anything, 'too high – he has to be reined in'. And the journalist Rob Hughes remembers seeing him in action at the Tottenham training ground. The physios had told him he could run around a bit, 'but no kicking'. 'So Gazza grabs a couple of apprentices and takes them off to the training pitch. And there he was, blasting shots at goal and giving his own running commentary: "Gazza's gonna hit this – it'll be a fucking massive shot," and so on. When he finished I asked him, "Does your leg hurt?" and he says, "Why, aye, it does a bit." So I tell him, "Stupid cunt" and his face crumples.'

This was in April 1992. In February, Gazza's wires and staples had been removed, and he was taken to Rome to watch the Lazio-Roma derby game – really to be shown off to the fans. The reception was ecstatic. With great ceremony he was led into the arena and there read from the cue card he'd been given: '*Arrive-derchee al prossimo campianato*' – to which he added: '*Ciao*'. The crowd went wild: 'Gazza's boys are here/Shag women and drink beer.' 'Unbelievable,' said Gazza; 'It's nice to be wanted again.'

By March, he was running, cycling, even kicking. And he had a new girlfriend, Sheryl Kyle – a married woman with two small children. 'He's had his fill of dolly birds,' the *People* was told by 'a friend': 'He wants to settle down. He likes Sheryl because she's stable, level-headed.' In April he played his first full practice match and performed reasonably well, though in slow motion. In May, Lazio was told that he was ready for inspection. The Italians sent a three-man delegation, and Gascoigne was subjected to six days of training-tests – sprints, jumps, twists and turns, five-a-side games and so on. He was then given the go-ahead for his final clinical examination in Rome. This was scheduled for late May, and Lazio had arranged for it to be conducted by an American sports-injury specialist, Jim Andrews. The transfer to Lazio would depend on Andrews's verdict.

The medical in Rome was an odd business. At first, Andrews announced that 'everything looks fine'. Then, having studied a scan of Gazza's knee, he said: 'It's fair to say we are undecided.' To which the Lazio doctor added:

'The images from the scan have underlined some problems.'
This was on 25 May. Next day, the verdict was rewritten.
At a press conference, Andrews declared that all was well.
Stress tests had removed the doubts raised by the scan: in
other words, the knee didn't look right but it worked. In
fact, Andrews put it more buoyantly than that: 'Paul
Gascoigne is quite simply a superman. A superman physi-
cally and a superman mentally.' If he continued to work
hard at his exercises, 'He will be great. Not mediocre, great,
perhaps the greatest.'

Some observers were puzzled. Why the change of mind?
Lazio expected to raise about ten million pounds from
season-ticket sales on the strength of Gascoigne's signing.
In Lazio's shop, 'Go Gazza' T-shirts were already selling at
ten pounds a time. The fans had been told to expect
miracles. The club had had a sorry season, President Calleri
had gone, and Dino Zoff, the coach, was having his car
stoned. In this atmosphere, the *idea* of a Gascoigne could
not lightly be abandoned. There were those who believed
that Lazio would have bought him even if he had been
crippled.

As it was, they were now able to hail him as 'the best
player in the world', 'the new Maradona', and 'the saviour
we've been waiting for'. When, on 27 May, Gascoigne at
last signed for Lazio, the team manager Maurizio Manzini
told the press: 'I feel like I did when I became a father for the
first time. I've been waiting for the baby and it's finally
arrived. And what a big baby it is!'

Actively Portly

W HEN IAN RUSH was asked to explain his failure to score goals for Juventus he replied that being in Italy was like being in a foreign country. And this rather happily summed up the attitude of at least fifty per cent of the British soccer stars who had taken the Italian plunge. In the words of Enzo Bearzot, the former Italian national team manager. Brits were notorious for '*i fallimenti, le fughe, i litigi, le sbronze*' – in other words, for reneging on contracts and for being quarrelsome and boozy. Not that liquor was a problem for Ian Rush: one of his chief gripes was that no one in Italy stocked his favourite brand of tea-biscuit.

Strange as it now seems, there are strong historical links between the football clubs of England and Italy. Genoa – the oldest Italian club – was started in 1893 by British immigrant workers and was originally called the Genoa Cricket and Athletic Club. The Italians were not allowed to join. They did turn up, though, to watch this peculiar new English game that used 'a ball as yet unseen in Italy, pumped full of air and kicked with the feet' – and they liked what they saw. They liked it very much. Within five years an Italian League was founded, with teams from Genoa, Milan and Turin, and some promising inter-city rivalries took root.

It was not long before every self-respecting Italian town had to have its own soccer club. If you wanted to be a mayor, or just an average big-shot, you were well-advised to look to the fortunes of your local side. The League's First Division grew so huge – at one point it had sixty-four members – that there was no chance of getting through the fixture list within a single season. In the 1910s, the structure was rationalized into something like its present shape – with promotion and relegation between small divisions – by the now-legendary Vittorio Pozzo. In 1929, Pozzo became national team manager and stayed in that post for twenty years. By the time he retired Italy was Europe's most admired footballing nation.

Pozzo, it was often noted by the English, learned everything he knew about 'calcio' on the terraces at Old Trafford. As a young man he worked for a few years as a language teacher in Lancashire. But in these early days, an English influence was something the Italian clubs took pride in: quite a few of them had English managers; one or two – including, to this day, Juventus – employed the suffix 'FC' (Football Club) rather than 'AC' (*Associazione Calcio*). And Genoa, in its centenary year, still uses its English name, even though under Mussolini it was made to call itself Genova.

In other words, we used to be such friends. This quasi-colonial relationship did not survive much beyond the 1920s. By then the Italians no longer needed us to tell them how to play, and we were making a performance out of standing aloof from the world stage. Now and again, the English national team would give the foreigners a thrashing, but through the 1930s we stoutly refused to take part in the so-called World Cup – which Italy won twice in that decade. The assumption was that we could easily win the thing if we thought it were worth winning.

And then came the Hungarians in 1953 – a six-three defeat at Wembley, where we had never lost before, then seven-one in Budapest. From this year of shame, a new orthodoxy would dominate our thinking. The aliens had learned a few tricks which we, because of our climate, physique and stern island integrity, might never choose to learn. We decided to play to our strengths, our superior gifts of character and stamina, our will to win. In time, we would learn how to compete with the East Europeans, the Germans and the Dutch; we would learn how to win the European Cup with teams that were just a notch or two above the average. But Italy, although we beat them now and then, would always remain out of reach, the sinister, dark Other: a Brazil that was too close to home.

Whenever our standing in Europe was discussed, Italy was the principal yardstick by which we measured our own strengths and weaknesses. Italians were more passionate about the game than we were but they were also, or therefore, more corrupt. They had flamboyant skills, but they were sneaky with their fouls, their connings of the referee, their intimidation ploys and so on. Their clubs were richer than ours, their rivalries more vehement, but this was only because they were owned by industrial chieftains and political hustlers who were using the game to promote themselves, their businesses or their careers. Our soccer may be down-at-heel but at least it was what it seemed to be: a working-class Saturday diversion with no compromising attachments to the toffs and megalomaniacs who controlled our weekday lives. You would see no mink or cashmere at our footballing first nights. Aptly enough, the fiasco at Tottenham was the result of aping 'continental' methods.

A similar sort of double-think was evident when we talked about the actual players. In the 1950s, when many of our prejudices on the matter first took shape, the British player was seen as an honest artisan, pinned down by a maximum wage of twenty pounds a week, no richer and no grander than the fans who watched him play. By comparison, the Italian was the rich kid, deeply spoiled. We heard of back-handers, under-the-counter pay-offs, fixed cup-ties, referees who could be bought – horrors unimaginable in our decently feudal dispensation. Their players were better-looking than ours, we had to concede – but didn't they just *know* it? There was a sickening narcissism in the way they stroked the ball around so prettily. And why were they always passing it backwards, or sideways? Why were they so scared to lose?

An explicit falling-out between Italy and England came in the late 1950s. The Italians had lifted their ban on importing foreign players, and the English, whose maximum-wage limit was still – just about – in place, were obvious first targets. The Italian agent became a regular, and disconcerting, presence at our football grounds, and the papers were full of rumours that this or that star player was about to succumb to the 'lure of the lira'. Players who showed signs of being tempted were vilified as avaricious and disloyal, and there was much patriotic glee whenever one of them came skulking back, full of complaints about excessive club discipline, foul business on the field and the lack of basic human amenities – like tea-biscuits or warm beer. We heard less about John Charles and Gerry Hitchens, players who signed for teams in Italy and performed well, than we did about malcontents like Dennis Law, Joe Baker and Jimmy Greaves: each of these was reckoned by the Italians to be of '*carratere turbulento*'.

In the case of Joe Baker, there was the strange business of a wrecked Alfa Romeo; with Dennis Law, there were regular punch-ups with photographers. Most difficult of all was Jimmy Greaves, whose turbulence came across as a protracted sulk. He had signed for Milan 'for mercenary reasons' – £5,000 a year plus a £15,000 signing-on fee – but shortly after his transfer had gone through, the English maximum-wage limit was abolished. 'It was like a sick joke,' said Greaves, 'only I couldn't see the funny side.' He wanted to leave Milan even before he arrived, and most of his time in Italy was spent trying to break a three-year contract. He stayed for four months and when he returned, to sign for Spurs, he was like a man who had been let out of jail.

Apart from the money vexation, Greaves's problem had been similar to that of Ian Rush – Italy was, irreparably, foreign. The Cockney sparrow had been sat on by the Italian eagle. In Milan, they couldn't make Greaves out: he seemed to them both dull and irresponsible. He objected to the club's system of '*ritiri*', by which players are taken off to a training camp for two nights before each game. Greaves wanted to stay at home with his wife. On other nights, though, he liked to be out on the town. His ale-house instincts were frowned on by his bosses and avidly scrutinized in the Italian soccer press. He was gated, suspended, fined, and, when he then asked to leave, the Milanese said no. In England we read about his plight with indignation: set our Jimmy free.

And when he did come back, his Italian saga was told and re-told, as an admonitory fable. With Law and Baker also set free, and with big money now on offer here at home, the Italians could be slandered without inhibition. It would be twenty years before the Anglo-Italian market re-opened for business. In the 1980s, there was another mini-exodus, but by then attitudes had changed, or were less stridently expressed. Graeme Souness, Trevor Francis, Liam Brady and Ray Wilkins were impressive on the field and sophisticated enough off it to make light of the tea-biscuit problem. They learned some rudimentary Italian – enough, anyway, to be described as 'fluent' in the English press – and were forthcoming with the Euro-chic.

When Gascoigne signed for Lazio, our most recent export to Italy had been David Platt. Platt had served a year with about-to-be-relegated Bari and had now joined Juventus for 1992–93. Some claimed that Juventus had bankrolled Platt's original transfer from Aston Villa and had arranged for him to serve an apprenticeship, or trial, at Bari. Similar rumours attached to Lazio's purchase of Paul Gascoigne, but they were always angrily denied in Rome.

In terms of image Platt was the opposite of Gazza. He was the clean-limbed head boy to Gascoigne's inky-thumbed delinquent. During his year at Bari, he had behaved flawlessly, praising the language, the weather, the people, the fashions. 'Armani, Valentino, even the names roll off the tongue,' he'd say, and the Italians loved it. He did not quite give off the sheen of an authentic *calcio*-celeb, and there was something rather badly wrong with his hairstyle, but he tried. 'Be it three or eight years, I wouldn't want to go back without saying I'd done more than just the football.'

At Juventus, known as the 'Old Lady' of Italian soccer, they set great store by what they called 'the Juventus Deportment'. In the words of their president: 'We conduct ourselves correctly. We set out to present an example of how to live in the sporting world.' Platt, always courteous, low-key and anxious to fit in, was clearly Juve material. Gascoigne, according to the evidence, was not. It was Gianni Agnelli, the owner of Juventus, who after the World Cup called Gazza 'a dog of war with the face of a child', but Agnelli then listened to his advisers. The word was that Gascoigne's deportment was not all that it might be, that he would clash with referees, or with provocative opponents, and be given the reddest of red cards.

And this was pretty much the view in England. When Gascoigne set off for Italy, the sages queued up to prophesy the worst. John Sadler of the *Sun* warned Gazza that 'If you muck about, become side-tracked by temptation, the future that was salvaged in the operating theatre won't be worth three coins in a fountain. You've been given your chance. Again. Don't blow it. Again.' Even Terry Venables feared that if Gascoigne failed to approach Italy 'in the widest possible way' he would be 'eaten alive'. Venables wanted him to learn the language and 'become part of the life of the city. If he is left to himself and begins to look in rather than out, and just surrounds himself with his own English friends, it could be a disaster.' There were words too from

Italy's most celebrated soccer hard-man, Claudio Gentile, now retired: 'If he uses the elbow on the pitch it will be the end of him . . . If he tries to make people look silly he will be seriously hurt. Italian defenders always get their revenge.'

Most specific of all, though, was the advice from Jimmy Greaves: 'If Gazza's experiences are going to be anything like mine, he will react to the iron discipline of Italian soccer by rebelling against the rule-makers. I turned into a rebel when AC Milan tried to restrict my private life, and I became expert at slipping past their bodyguards to sneak into local bars for a drink or three. I was disciplined enough not to get legless, but it was the pressures of Italian soccer that made me start drinking as a habit rather than a hobby.'

Gascoigne was leaving the green playing fields of England for the 'minefields' of Italian soccer; he had a mountain – an 'Italian Alp' – to climb; he was about to be thrown to 'the lions of Rome'. Even as the papers issued these warnings they found time to outline the rewards that lay in store. In *Today*, we were given – by the aptly-named Ben Bacon – a breakdown of Gazza's '£10 million Italian Job'. His basic salary, said Bacon, would be three million pounds over five years, 'but his total package from Lazio amounts to nearly £5 million.' And this would be doubled by 'world-wide endorsements'. The bonuses for playing well would be 'staggering' – £90,000 per man if Lazio qualified for the UEFA Cup; £200,000 each if they won the Championship.

And this was just the money. Gazza's 'lifestyle' would be similarly 'swish': he would be getting a 'top-of-the-range Mercedes' and 'an elegant, exquisitely furnished villa' with 'a lake nearby where he can fish to escape the intolerable pressure he will be under'. Bacon had not himself laid eyes on this well-furnished villa but he was able to provide photographs of 'one of the villas Paul Gascoigne has seen' and of 'picturesque Formello', a suburb twenty kilometres from central Rome, and 'home to the rich and famous' – the captions read 'super-bia' and 'Rome sweet Rome'. All this, in Bacon's view, might well prove too much for 'the kid who was brought up on brown ale in a working men's club in Dunston.' To help him cope, Gazza would have in residence his younger brother Carl, and once a month 'dad John will come out for a week to check on his boy.'

Gascoigne's pickings would indeed be rich, though not as rich as they would have been if he had not wrecked his knee. His £10,000 a week was just over half of what he was originally offered. Des Walker had gone to Sampdoria for twice as much. And Villa Gazza, wherever it turned out to be, was not going to come cheap. Gascoigne would be 'making a contribution' to the rent. By Italian standards, said the *Independent*, his would be a 'journeyman's salary'. Ruud Gullit of Milan was on a million pounds a year.

'This is Rome, right, but where's Lazio?' asked Gazza as he stood outside the Lazio club shop in Rome's Via Farini. His bodyguard Giovanni Zeqireya explained that 'Rome is city, Lazio is region.'

'But you're a Lazio supporter, right?'

'Oh, yes.' Zeqireya seemed to be an asset: six foot three in his shades, a karate champion and one-time protector of Madonna and Stallone, he also managed to look kindly and long-suffering. And he had undoubtedly taken to Gazza:

'The thing about Paul is that although he may look like a man, inside he is a boy.'

A dog of war with the face of a child. Perhaps this would turn out to be the key: this childishness that everyone at home was urging Gascoigne to outgrow. 'He loves children,' said Zeqireya. 'That is not just very important but to an Italian it says a lot about the person.' Poor Gazza: he always seemed to be on the lookout for adoptive parents, for wise uncles and stand-in older brothers, for shoulders he could cry on. In London Terry Venables and Mel Stein had fitted the bill, and in their different ways each would continue to look out for him, but they could no longer be on twenty-four-hour call. During his early negotiations with Lazio, Gascoigne had an agreement with Glenn Roeder, his former captain at Newcastle and always a shrewd and imperious presence on the field, that he would move to Rome and serve as an all-purpose minder, a supplier of day-to-day 'maturity', but Roeder now had other plans. Brother Carl and dad John would bring with them an authentic whiff of Dunston, but to judge from appearances they would be looking to Gazza to take care of *them*.

Then there was girlfriend Sheryl, now in mid-divorce from her husband. The hacks had not quite made up their minds about Sheryl. Was she just another bimbo or was she middle class, a cut above? There was the estate-agent husband, the Hertfordshire semi, the children with fancy names – Mason and Bianca. For the moment, the papers decided to portray her as would-be genteel. When she and Gascoigne took a holiday in Florida before he flew to Rome, the *Sun* went too. Sheryl, they divined, had envisaged a romantic twosome. Alas, though, Gazza had turned up with his Dunston tribe: 'Dad John, mum Carol, brother Carl, two sisters and their boyfriends and drinking pal Five-Bellies Gardner.' All the boys, including Gazza, had had their heads shaved, or re-shaved, for the trip and from day one they engaged enthusiastically with all the local spots: there were 'high-spirited' nights out in the 'British-run London Tavern' and 'boozy jaunts' to Disneyworld. Sheryl, according to a 'family friend', was an 'outsider' in all this and was 'getting the cold shoulder' from the lads. 'She didn't have a great time,' said the friend. 'She never expected to land up with five skinheads – it's not her scene.'

This being so, it was just as well that she did not attend Gascoigne's farewell 'do' in Dunston a week later. STRIP GIRLS WHIP GAZZA – SHOCK SCENES AT HIS FAREWELL was the *Sun*'s front-page exclusive on 5 July. Two hundred guests had gathered at the Excelsior to send Gazza on his way, and the organizers had thoughtfully laid on two kissogram girls. 'Gazza was lost for words' when 'scantily clad six-footer' Lindsay Nesbitt removed her nurse's uniform to reveal 'just a black basque, stockings and suspenders'. 'He just looked around, really shy,' said one witness. 'Nothing like you'd expect.' But Lindsay had her way: 'She got him on his knees and made him twang her suspenders with his teeth. All his mates and family were cheering.' Then came the whipping: Gazza, Carl and Five-Bellies were 'each told to bend over and were then whipped ten times by a "roly-polygram" '. Was this the girl or the instrument? We were not told. At the end, with everyone 'fairly drunk', Gazza gave his goodbye speech: 'I can't go to London or Italy to enjoy mesel'. So I come here to Dunston and the Excelsior where nobody pesters me. I'm going away on Tuesday but I'll see you again at Christmas when I've done the business and taken the piss out of the Italians.' The speech was greeted with chants of 'Dunston! Dunston!'

When Gascoigne left England in July he was seriously overweight – actively portly, one might say. The Italians took one look and set to work. For the first time, the Lazio trainers and physios had sole charge of their expensive property. The season started on 6 September, and there was not much chance that Gazza would be ready. But even if he were to be ready, there was the question of how Lazio would use him. Under Italian rules, a club is allowed to field three foreigners, no more. Milan, for example, had half a dozen costly imports, at least three of whom – Papin? Boban? Savicevic? – would start the season on the bench. Lazio would also have to choose: in addition to Gascoigne, it had Karl-Heinz Riedle and Thomas Doll from Germany, and Aron Winter from Holland. Doll had been signed a year earlier, after Gazza's injury at Wembley, and Winter was recruited when it became clear that the Englishman's rehabilitation might run into the new season. Each was a distinguished international and had cost Lazio big money.

Italian commentators were already hinting that some unpleasantness could be expected. Thomas Doll was said to have declared that if he and Gascoigne played together, he would not surrender the number 8 shirt that he had worn the year before. Gascoigne could have the number 10. In 1991–92, Doll had been Lazio's star player. An East German, he was known to delight in his Italian celebrity and in all the consumer goodies that went with it. It was said that his car was comically over-equipped with electronic gadgetry. He wore his blond hair long and wavy and he had a ready smile. One could guess that he might not be overjoyed by the arrival of a new messiah. Had he not served as the club's saviour for a year, a year in which Gascoigne – through his own folly – had been stretched out on the treatment table? Was it his fault that the club had finished tenth?

Not so long ago, Lazio would have been content with a mid-table slot in *Serie A*. In their ninety-two-year history, the club had only twice won major honours – the Cup in 1958, the Championship in 1974. They had served time in Italy's Division Two. In England they were barely known before the Gascoigne transfer. For most English fans, the name Lazio evoked vague memories of an ugly clash with Arsenal in the UEFA Cup some twenty years ago, when a punch-up developed at the post-match dinner, with players and officials piling in. 'Too much wine,' said Lazio's coach, who had been in the thick of the fighting. 'If my players go crazy it is not my fault.'

In Rome, the brawl with Arsenal would have surprised nobody. Of the city's two clubs, Lazio was known to be the home of roughnecks. And it had a guilty past. Its support came mainly from the rural areas around Rome and from what was left of the old fascist aristocracy. In smart Roman circles, no one would want to be caught preferring 'Mussolini's team' to their rivals, the newer and more successful AS Roma. Most of the slogans and obscenities that deface the city's walls and statues are pro-Lazio, and some have a racist slant. Several celebrate the *Ultras* or *Irriducibili*,

Lazio's hooligan squads, would-be counterparts to the head-bangers of Millwall and West Ham. The term *Irriducibili* means 'the indomitables', or 'those who will not yield'.

Although Lazio and Roma play on alternate weeks at the same stadium – the Stadio Olympico – the Lazio bumpkins have more miles to travel than Roma's city slickers. Hence, maybe, the gang instinct, the feeling they seem to have that they are invading their own city, a city 'occupied' by AS Roma. For the *Irriducibili*, Gazza and his Geordie boys were kindred spirits, and they were ready to worship this *ragazzaccio*, or 'rude boy'. For them, tales of Gascoigne's indiscipline were welcomed as testimonials, and in their slogans and banners they were keen to let *Il Matto* know that, if he wanted rough company in Rome, he need look no further than the Curva Nord – the Olympico's North Bank.

This was not quite the image that Societa Sportiva Lazio itself had been fostering in recent years, and the new regime – under the presidency of Sergio Cragnotti, a merchant banker and packaging magnate – was seemingly rich enough to force the club up-market. In the close season, a Lazio buying spree had brought in not just Gascoigne from England and Aron Winter from Holland but also a trio of Italian big names: Roberto Cravero from Torino, Diego Fuser from Milan and Giuseppe Signori from Foggia. The coach, Dino Zoff, was Italy's captain and goalkeeper when they won the World Cup in '82. So far, Zoff's managerial career had not been much of a success – at Juventus he had won nothing, and Lazio, during his two years, had failed to break into the top half of the table. With his new signings,

Zoff was expected to deliver – not this year, perhaps, but soon.

The fitness was of course what mattered most. It was more than fifteen months now since Gascoigne had played competitive football. In two practice games, he had shown the old touch at odd moments, but he was blowing hard before the end and complaining of muscular twinges – not in the bad knee but here and there, mostly in the thigh. In one of the games, for Lazio's reserves against the first team, he scored a goal and then shortly afterwards almost crippled another of Zoff's new boys, the Under-21 international Giuseppe Favalli. Zoff, according to one report, gave Gazza a dressing-down 'in his best pidgin'.

When Lazio kicked off the new season against Sampdoria, Gascoigne did not attend the game: 'I get too upset just watching.'

'Where were you, Gazza?' asked the *Mirror* man, 'out shopping?'

'No, I was at home, looking to make babies,' was the pert reply. Two days later, Gascoigne flew to Santander to join the England team in its preparation for a friendly against Spain. Graham Taylor wanted him to 're-acclimatize'. He also believed that Gazza's presence might give the lads a lift – a lift they badly needed after their dismal showing in the summer's European Nations Cup. This reunion in Spain was the English reporters' first chance of a Gazza close-up since he'd left for Italy two months before.

How was the leg? they asked.

It was just fine, except that 'the right leg doesn't bend as far as the left. It stretches a certain muscle in your leg, and the muscle has been very hard lately. Every time I kick a ball – it's three times now – I split the thigh. I can run. I can do everything, but I'm not kicking with my right foot at the moment.'

Most days he didn't think about the leg. 'All I know is that I want to give everything I have for England again.' He had thrown away his World Cup videos, he said. In the 'dark days' he would watch an England tape 'and upset mesel' all over again. I watched David Platt's last-minute winner against Belgium. I thought it might help. It didn't. Just made it worse. I've missed it all so much. English voices, the banter, the jokes. Yes, I have been lonely.'

What about Italy? How was he doing with the language?

'There was a dog barking outside my house. It kept on and on. I shouted at it in English but it kept on. So I went through my phrase book looking for something like "Shut up". I yelled out *"Silenzio, bastardo"* and it stopped.' In other words, no problem. The hacks were greatly charmed and next day they reported warmly on Gazza's impressive weight loss, his charisma, his new-found maturity. They had grown tired of Graham Taylor-bashing for the moment: a reborn Gascoigne would be more than welcome. But what *about* the knee?

Under a clause in Gascoigne's transfer deal, Lazio and Tottenham were committed to play two exhibition games, one in London, one in Rome. The Rome date had been twice postponed, since without Gascoigne the game would not have much point. It was now scheduled for 23 September, and after much further hesitation Lazio announced that this would now for certain be Gazza's *'giorno della verità'*, his day of truth. In London, not long before, we had sat through a Channel 4 television film called *Gazza: The Fightback* in which we had watched the saw tearing at the kneebone, the scalpel scooping out the tissue. We had seen Gascoigne's X-certificate X-rays, his livid six-inch scar. We had seen him taking his first nervous steps after the wires and screws had been removed. The idea of this fragile reconstruction getting clattered by a first-division tackle made at least one of his fans shudder. Still, let it be remembered that the first tackle, when it came, would very likely be a *Spurs* tackle: it might not connect.

Finally Fit

O N THE DAY before the Spurs game, Gascoigne was being interviewed by Gordon Burn for an *Esquire* cover story – a story for which the magazine was asked to pay £5,000 plus £3,000-worth of Armani gear. 'I want them to play that song,' Burn overheard Gascoigne tell Mel Stein before the match. 'Phil Collins. "I can feel it comin' in the air tonight . . ." Remember. Tell them.'

Burn did not get many other pearls in exchange for his, or *Esquire's*, cash. As with most interviews with Gazza, the main drift was to do with how much Gazza hated giving interviews. And on this day he had a particular new grievance. An Italian magazine, *Eva Express*, had snapped a topless Sheryl Kyle sunbathing in the grounds of Villa Gazza. The pictures had been sold on to English tabloids. The Italians billed their exclusive feature '*Nudo nel "Ritiro" Privato*', but it was the English Gascoigne blamed: 'You expect that from the English. Who are they? What do they do? They're nothing. They get paid for writing crap, following people around and getting pissed up. That's all.'

Gordon Burn took this on the chin. He had, he reported, been pleasantly surprised by the new-style, Romanized Paul Gascoigne: 'I came half-expecting to see somebody spraying effluent from both ends, like some bloated grotesque in *Viz*.' For *Esquire*'s photoshoot, Gazza was looking pretty good: 'composed, calm, muscles toned, jawline firm, almost languorous'. And he was proud of his trim figure, although, 'There's no way I was ever the size people thought. The English papers used to touch the pictures up to look fatter.'

At the Lazio training ground, Gazza's conduct was more reassuringly *Viz*-like. 'Yiz fifteen great poofs, yiz!' he bellowed at his team-mates as they limbered up. And he clearly preferred being photographed to being asked: 'Do you still believe that scoring a goal is more thrilling than "shooting your bolt"?'

'I've forgotten what scoring a goal is like,' was his reply.

The small concrete stand that overlooks the practice area was filled with English newsmen. When one was caught eavesdropping as Gascoigne spoke to Italian television, the player turned on him: 'I've told you,' he said, 'if you take notes now, I won't talk to you later.' This was petulant, but who could blame him? He recognized some of the faces in the stand. He knew that these men had come to bury him or praise him. He was on edge, under scrutiny. Dino Zoff was not happy with his player's pre-match mood: 'I hope it doesn't all become too exciting and emotional for him.'

On 23 September, *il giorno della verità*, Rome had its first rainfall for six weeks. On the day I arrived, just an hour before Lazio and Tottenham were scheduled to do battle, there was lightning and great rolls of thunder. By kick-off time there was a crowd of about 25,000 in the cavernous Stadio Olympico – a remarkable turnout, given that the national side was playing a Swiss team live on television at the same time. But few of us had thought to bring umbrellas. By eight-thirty, the rain was sheeting down, and the thunder and lightning seemed to be directly overhead. The police dogs around the track began to bark. Were lions whelping in the street? Had Gazza been *too* saucy with the gods?

Like Phil Collins, I too could feel it in the air tonight. And so too could the *Irriducibili*, massed on the Curva Nord, their Union Jacks grotesquely on display. The huge screens at each end of the ground showed gems from Gazza's past as well as his pop video, 'Fog on the Tyne', to which the *Irriducibili* gamely tried to sing along. More thunder. When the teams finally came running out, to an enormous cheer, there were some silent and anxious-looking spectators in the VIP box: dad John, mum Carol, brother Carl, Sheryl, Mel Stein and Lawrie McMenemy, England's assistant manager. And on the Spurs bench we could see Dave Butler and John Sheridan, the physios who for twelve months had worked on Gascoigne's knee. Sheridan was in tears before the game: it had been a long wait, he said, but he had never doubted that the day would come.

And there was Gazza, centre stage, the number 10, saluting the North Bank. Thomas Doll was wearing 8. Lazio's selection problem had been simplified by Aron Winter's absence, playing for Holland against Norway. As the players lined up for the start, we Spurs fans for the first time checked 'our' line-up. It was deeply unfamiliar. None of Gazza's best mates was in the team, apart from Steve Sedgley and the goalkeeper, Ian Walker. No Gary Mabbutt, no Paul Allen. And there was a sprinkling of kids we'd barely heard of: Nick Barmby, playing his first game for Tottenham; Ian Hendon; Andy Turner. We hoped that these teenagers knew what tonight was all about, that they wouldn't try too hard to cut a dash. In defence, Spurs had Ruddock and Cundy, two gorillas and, so far as we knew, no friends of Gazza: they had arrived at Spurs after he had left. We hoped that they too knew what was required of them: i.e. not very much.

As soon as play started, all eyes were on Gascoigne. He was running smoothly, that marvellous, high-chested run, and he was calling for the ball as if he really wanted it. It took him two minutes to get a touch, a neat lay-off, and seconds later he made a dart along the right wing and aimed a perfect cross to Stroppa, who headed into Walker's arms. A murmured '*Bella*, Gazza, *bella*' came from two rows back. Could we relax now, please? He was running, he could kick, his skill had not deserted him. And he seemed to be pacing himself sensibly, not moving forward every time Lazio attacked. During the first ten minutes he touched the ball eight times. Only once did he attempt a run at Tottenham's defence, and it was good to see Ruddock and Cundy respectfully backtracking. We could take about half an hour of this, we reckoned, and then Lazio could pull him off, point proved, no damage done. We might even settle down to watch the game.

And then Gascoigne, as if he'd sensed some slackening of terrace tension, turned the screw. A cross from Doll missed Riedle and ran loose to Gazza, six yards out, with no one near him. He did a little skip as he ran on to it, to get in stride, and that was that: a goal in the eleventh minute of his comeback. Gazza kept running, and the crowd behind the goal heaved forward. 'The fans sucked me to them,' he said later, and that's how it looked. *En route*, pursued by a small posse of ball-boys, photographers and cameramen, he had to swerve to avoid the track's water-jump. Five of his pursuers were less nimble and fell in. Back on the field, the Spurs team watched, all smiles, and in the VIP box there were hugs and tears. And we at last were able to sit back.

Or were we? When play resumed, Gascoigne was still beaming and his fists were clenched. The fear now was that he might think that this was all too easy and do something stupid. After a few minutes, though, he was positioning himself even more cautiously than at the start, as if he knew that the night's work was done, and done perfectly, and ought not to be spoiled. For the next half-hour, he made no real effort to keep up with play. Most of the time he hovered near the centre circle and waited for the ball to come to him. Just before the interval, as if fearing that perhaps his time was up, he tried one of his famous surges from midfield, holding off Jason Cundy and then Carl Tuttle, who grabbed at Gascoigne's shirt. The run ended with a weakish shot, and with both Tuttle and Gascoigne on the floor. But it was Tuttle who needed the trainer. As Gazza picked himself up, Riedle and Stroppa came across to remonstrate: don't push it, seemed to be the drift. Gazza pretended to look hangdog but as the teams came off at half-time he was looking, as he'd say, well chuffed. That late run was something that he'd *had* to try. And he had scored the only goal.

Zoff gave him twenty minutes of the second half, and Gazza made the most of them: an intelligent through-pass to Doll created Lazio's second goal, from Stroppa. But Gazza was looking sluggish now, worn out, and made no complaint when he was summoned to the bench. For

Paul Gascoigne with Vinnie Jones, 1988.

Paul Gascoigne: England v Cameroon in the World Cup 1990.

Gascoigne after England's 5-4 defeat to Germany in the 1990 World Cup semi-final.

Returning from the World Cup.

Gascoigne with Margaret Thatcher.

Gascoigne with Sheryl Kyle.

Gascoigne being stretchered off during the 1991 FA Cup Final.

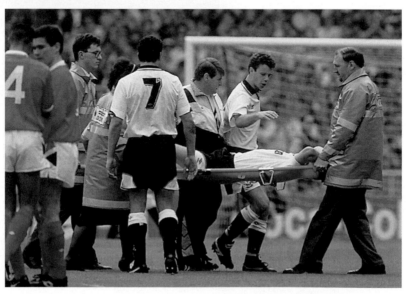

Leaving the Princess Grace Hospital in London with a new cruciate ligament.

Being helped from Walkers Night Club, his kneecap broken.

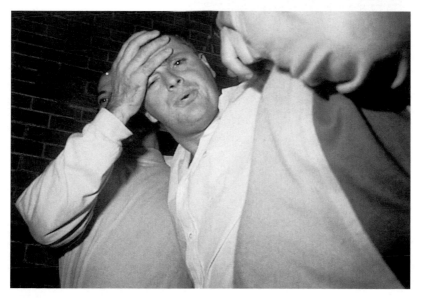

Arriving in Rome, August 1991.

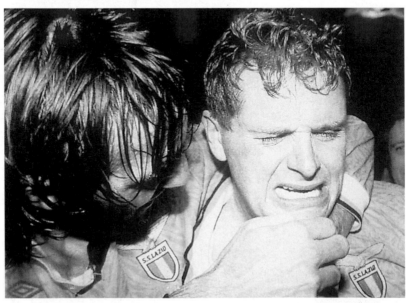

In tears following his goal against Roma.

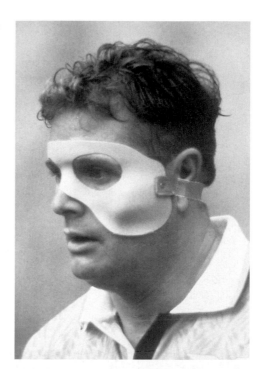

Wearing his protective face mask.

Gascoigne the Glasgow Orangeman.

Gascoigne plus new friends: Chris Evans and Danny Baker.

Gascoigne expelled: May 31, 1998.

the rest of the ninety minutes he horsed around with the thirty or so photographers who crowded round the dugout. Play went on uneventfully until near the end when the Italians got a third, and Gazza's antics were the focus of attention. He ran through his entire funny-man routine: the stuck-out tongue, the wincing-manic grin. He threw a flagon of water over a photographer who got too close, and this won him a huge cheer. And when the final whistle came, he was instantly back on the field, bear-hugging and arm-waving, shaking hands with everyone in sight. And then, to cap it all, he set off on a triumphal trot to the brink of a wildly-welcoming North Bank: *re per una notte*, as the papers said next day. King for a night.

'*Oh yes, à proprio Paul*' ('It's really Paul') was another Italian headline, and in England it was 'Emperor of Rome!' In theatrical terms, the night had been splendidly successful, and the reviews were suitably ecstatic. But everybody knew that the real test was yet to come. The Spurs game had been the friendliest of friendlies. On the following Sunday, Lazio would be facing Genoa at home. Should Gascoigne play? Cragnotti, the club's owner, had no doubts. He told reporters that 'It would be nice if Zoff could find a way to use Gazza even if it isn't for the full ninety minutes.' And then again, more forcefully: 'Surely Zoff will not waste the chance to play this new champion we have with us. It's very clear he wants to play and needs to play.'

The next day the champion himself announced that he felt 'ready to play' and that between now and Sunday he would be making cups of tea for Dino Zoff and cleaning all his shoes. Zoff was, as usual, poker-faced, not telling, but it was evident that, left to himself, he would hold Gascoigne back, at least for a few weeks. But Cragnotti had spoken, and Zoff had to reply. The problem was: who to leave out? Winter had been performing well, and Thomas Doll, when asked if he thought Gascoigne would play against Genoa, had simply said: 'I play.'

Zoff tried to stall, saying that if Gascoigne missed the Genoa match, he would certainly be picked for the following week's fixture, against Parma. But this was not good enough, for Cragnotti, for the fans, or for the English pressmen who were hanging on in Rome. My own return ticket was a seven-day job. I had to stay in Rome. I might even get to look at a few buildings. Or I could make a trip to the Via Britannia in search of a bar that had been opened there in Gazza's honour by a consortium of ageing Irreducibles. Rumour had it that Five-Bellies worked there as a barman – unpaid: he liked the atmosphere. The bar was called Wembley Park Station, and when I finally did seek it out, I had evidently chosen the wrong night – the place was empty. No Five-Bellies, no customers. On the walls there were pictures of unidentified English players of the 1950s, and hanging from the ceiling were scarves and rosettes of English clubs, from Preston to Notts County. These, too, were seriously out of date. The manager asked me if I knew anyone in London who might want to buy the joint, cut-price. I asked him if he thought Zoff should pick Gascoigne against Genoa. Oh yes, was the reply. Wembley Park Station badly needed a fit Gazza.

Gascoigne had now relaxed the policy of 'silenzio' (not speaking to the press) which had been intermittently in force since his arrival. 'I would like to show the fans my best but I do need to get match-fit. The only way to do that is to play.' And so he played, at the expense of Winter, who did not protest.

For me, the ordeal of watching the Tottenham game was child's play compared to Lazio versus Genoa, just four days later. This time the opposition needed points and, so far as we knew, had no particular compassion for our wounded star. And Gascoigne's approach this time was likely to be different. Against Tottenham he had answered Question One: was he still able to play football? It was time now for Question Two. And sure enough, right from the start, he was striving to 'show the fans my best', to let them know that he was special. He shuffled and dummied in tight corners; he made a couple of bold runs at the Genoa defence; and when he passed the ball, he opted always for the imaginative angle, now and then outsmarting his own colleagues.

None of it worked quite as Gazza would have wished, but in a way this didn't matter. The fans were afforded intimations of what a fully fit Gascoigne might be like. They saw the body-swerve, the on-a-sixpence ninety-degree turn; they saw the acceleration and the power. In glimpses, maybe, but sufficient to ignite their fantasies. The crowd of 50,000 cheered everything he tried. And if his team-mates were aggrieved they did not show it. When a pass was over-hit or when Gazza juggled himself into trouble, none of them complained. Doll even put himself in the way of a tackle that was meant for Gascoigne.

Were the Genoa defenders giving the Englishman an inch or two in which to show his wares? In or near their own area they were unbending but once or twice in midfield or on the touchline they could have clobbered him but didn't. Or was this my anxious fancy? Just before the end of the first half, Gascoigne was caught from behind and went down, clutching at his knee. The stadium fell silent as the Lazio trainers and medics gathered round. Gazza had one hand across his eyes and with the other he was prodding at the doctor's leg: to show him where it hurt. We waited for the stretcher to appear, the ambulance, the Wembley re-run, but suddenly the crowd around him cleared and he was on his feet, attempting a few experimental hops, then running, with a limp. The whistle blew: half-time. As the teams walked off, three Genoa players were at Gazza's side, as if to commiserate, and from the crowd there was an uncertain flutter of applause. He was still limping when he disappeared into the tunnel.

Gascoigne did not appear for the second half, but we thought we could see him on the bench. Lazio had two other light-haired players – Doll and Sclosa – but they were on the pitch. It had to be Gazza. If so, he was sitting very still. After the game, the Lazio club doctor announced that all was well, that we had had a false alarm: 'It wasn't a big accident. Paul was hit on the knee around the sciatic nerve, but there is no distortion of the knee joint. The impact deadened his leg for a moment. He was a little scared. But he will have to get accustomed to these kinds of kicks.'

Gascoigne refused to comment. He had reimposed his 'silenzio', he said later on television, because the papers had told lies about a 'quarrel' he had never had with Dino Zoff. 'It's the lies I canna stand,' he told Channel 4, to whom he was contracted. Even so, the papers contrived to get some quotes, of the 'he told friends' variety: 'I was scared for a moment but it's not serious. The thing I remember most was how quiet the crowd went. The lad who hit me came up at half-time and said he was sorry. He thought he'd only tapped me.'

By the following Tuesday, Gascoigne was back in training, and Zoff was hinting that he might pick him for Sunday's game against Parma. Zoff looked depressed when he said it, but Zoff always looked depressed. As Joe Lovejoy of the *Independent* wrote: 'The sighs of relief could be heard all the way from Lazio to Lancaster Gate.' Nonetheless, the incident was troubling. Two years ago such a tackle would probably not have found its mark: Gazza would have sensed it in advance and twisted clear. But he had lingered for a second, wholly focused on the man in front of him. Then thwack – he was taken from behind. And, whatever he may be saying to his friends, he *had* been badly scared. This was his first competitive collision for almost eighteen months, and it had made his knee go numb. How could he not be scared? From now on, would his evasive instincts quicken or would his every move be tinged with apprehension? The two might amount to the same thing, of course, and anyway such questions were absurdly premature, but we too had had a nasty fright. Would watching Gazza always be like this? As the club doctor said, he would have to get used to the kicks, and so would we. But how?

Gascoigne did play against Parma and for thirty minutes he played well. He came off midway through the second half, triumphant and unscathed. And Lazio, who had drawn all their games so far, at last came good. They won five-two.

93

Gazza helped to make two of the goals and he won a penalty from which Signori scored. For the penalty, he was rudely felled by Taffarel, the Parma goalie, but this time there was no deathly hush. Gazza cheerfully bounced to his feet. Indeed, throughout the game, his demeanour seemed determinedly bubbly and fear-free, as if he had become weary of our worries. And on the bench, after he was substituted, he was seen to be 'back to his old self'. NUTS, said the *Daily Mirror*, over a big picture of Gazza playfully cupping the bits and bobs of one of his Lazio team-mates: 'He's still a mischievous ball-boy at heart – Gazza's certainly getting to grips with Italian football.'

Gazza's high jinks may have been aimed at Graham Taylor, who was sitting in the stand. Taylor had missed the Spurs and Genoa games but – apart from the injury scare – he had had good reports from McMenemy. After the Parma match he was able to pronounce: 'For the first thirty minutes we had glimpses of the old Gazza.' Would he then think of picking Gascoigne for England's forthcoming game with Norway – a vital World Cup qualifier to be played in ten days' time? To general astonishment, Taylor did not rule it out, though he doubted that Gascoigne would last ninety minutes.

Taylor had developed a Bobby Robson-like habit of giving voice to his every indecision and dilemma. He had begun his reign with expansive talk about the need for a new openness, for a cordial give-and-take with the journalists who had hounded Robson out of office. At first, the press had gone along with this, although there was no real warmth in their response. Where Bobby Robson, in defeat, had had the good grace to look haggard and distraught, Taylor was invariably ready with some verbose explanation. After the event, he had a way of talking about defeat as though it were a victory for pragmatic common sense: 'Well, Sweden of course won because they play the English game.' And he would say this with a strange, condescending fervour. At press conferences he was like a headmaster on parents' day: there was a touch of the bogus in his bonhomie.

Some thought there was a touch of envy too in his dealings with star players, players he could not think of as his own. Waddle and Beardsley had been too eagerly discarded, and Taylor's treatment of Lineker in the match against Sweden was surely both petty and vindictive. It was Gary's last game for his country, he was one short of an all-time scoring record, and Taylor pulled him off with twenty minutes to go. Had he forgotten Lineker's last-minute goal against Poland, the goal that got us to Sweden in the first place? No, Taylor was not the straight-arrow nice guy that he liked to seem.

There were also questions about his competence. Post-Sweden, the feeling was that for all his coaching-manual glibness, Taylor was probably out of his depth. He was a tactical ditherer, switching from one system to another. At heart he was a long-ball man. As a club manager, his success had been built on by-passing the midfield. At international level, though, he was obliged to present himself as a wily, sophisticated strategist. No wonder his players often seemed confused.

Certainly Graham Taylor was not Gascoigne's sort of boss. He was more social worker than adoptive parent.

There was something about Gazza that he badly wanted to sort out, once and for all. But this was no time for therapy. After the European Nations Cup fiasco in Sweden, where England had failed to win a game, Taylor's head was on the block. A defeat in the World Cup by Norway might well bring down the axe. For weeks he had been cooling the pro-Gascoigne fever, pronouncing wisely on the need for patience, pointing out that Gazza would need several full-length outings before he would be fit for the demands of the World Cup. 'I have to cut through the emotion,' he had said. 'I have to remember that the boy has not played for seventeen months, and no one, not even Paul Gascoigne, can make up for that.'

On the whole, the press had backed him: it would be mad to take the risk. By 13 October, though, most papers had already changed their tune. They had watched Gascoigne train at Bisham Abbey and declared him to be 'full of running again and back to peak fitness'. He had come out first in a short-sprint competition and had scored well in his lung-capacity tests. And there was more approving talk of his 'maturity', even after he replied: 'Fuck off, Norway,' to a television request for a message to that nation. This kind of conduct was, said Taylor, the 'downside' of Paul Gascoigne. 'His language at times! You think, "Oh, my God," but that's what makes these people . . . the Bothams, the Gascoignes. Most of us like to say the right thing, be diplomatic. He says what he feels.'

The news, finally, that Gazza would be playing at Wembley after all, added 30,000 to the gate, and on the morning of the game there were 'England Expects' war cries in the tabloids:

GIVE US BACK OUR PRIDE, GAZZA, said the *Mirror*; GO GET 'EM GAZZA said the *Sun*.

In the first half, Gazza did next to nothing – in fact, it was ten minutes before he got a kick. He had been given a 'free role', Taylor had told us, with the ferocious Ince and Batty detailed to protect him. Not much protection was required. For most of the time, Gazza was to be seen wandering in space a yard or two behind the front men, Wright and Shearer. England's passes from defence were high and inaccurate; rarely was it evident who they were meant for. The tall Norwegians had no trouble heading them back where they had come from. Time and again, Gascoigne was left standing as the ball flew over him, from end to end. He seemed to be under orders to stay forward; or at any rate not to seek the ball in his own half. In the first forty-five minutes, apart from one or two nice touches, his most notable contribution was to get booked for elbowing a Norwegian in the face.

By half-time, the England fans had stopped chanting Gascoigne's name and had settled into that old Wembley state of mind: a sort of placid discontent. The assumption was that Gazza would be substituted, that he had not after all been ready. But at least he was unharmed. There was a cheer, though, when he came out for the second half. If he had more to give, then so did we. And for eight minutes of that second half he delivered what we craved: a flashback to Italia '90. His control, his running with the ball, his passing were suddenly spot-on, and magisterial. He was upbraiding his team-mates when they made mistakes, snarling at the crowd for more support, demanding the ball whenever it came near. Play quickened and both teams looked springier, more urgent. And Gazza was red in the face, eyes popping, his neck-muscles at full pulse. For those few moments, we forgot the knee.

Gazza did not score the England goal, but it was his quick thinking that helped to set it up. The captain Stuart Pearce was shaping to take a free kick out near the right touch-line when Gascoigne yelled at him to wait. The foul had happened at least five yards further in. The ref agreed, the ball was moved forward and Pearce was now within range of Norway's goal. He unleashed one of his specials, Platt deflected it and England were one up. A minute later, Gazza planted a low, in-swinging corner-kick on Shearer's head, and it should have been two-nil.

By the time Ekdal equalized in the seventy-sixth minute, Gazza's fiesta had burned out. He played the last minutes at half-speed. But Taylor left him on until the end: his first full game since his return. And although England had dropped a vital point, perhaps *the* vital point, no one at the time seemed too concerned. The official man-of-the-match award, we heard as we trooped off into the night, had been given to Paul Gascoigne.

The following morning the papers were on a Gazzamanic high. Gascoigne's display had 'defied logic, medical opinion and shot to pieces any doubts about his ability to withstand the most intimidating challenges.' By the weekend, though, the plaudits for Gazza gave way to some pretty sour analyses of England's overall performance. Was Gascoigne really as wondrous as he seemed, or was it just that the men around him were so mediocre?

Hugh McIlvanney in the *Observer* was unillusioned: 'Have we been so institutionalised by the recent diet of workhouse gruel that we are prepared to burst into rapturous applause at the first taste of something more palatable?' Gascoigne was 'nothing less than a helping of caviare', but even he – 'every inch a player of the first rank' – had been ridiculously over-praised. There was that ugly foul to be remembered, as well as a need for 'that old bugbear, perspective'. If Bobby Charlton 'had done precisely the things that Gascoigne did on Wednesday he would not have been praised to anything like the same extent . . . Charlton had to perform in an era when failing to destroy the likes of Norway guaranteed a storm of disapproval.'

There was justice in McIlvanney's scorn. England had been inspired by Gazza for ten minutes but otherwise their play was unimpressive, both frantic and laborious – an unlikely combination but one for which the English are renowned. On the other hand, Gascoigne had shown – as in the World Cup – that team spirit could be lifted by the performance of one player. He had shown too that his own spirit could be lifted. The crowd's oaths and chants were familiar music to his ears; his team-mates revered him as their leader; the hype was in a language he could understand.

For McIlvanney, Gazza at Wembley was a 'rose among wallflowers'. If, just four days later, he had watched Lazio against Milan, his point would have been proved. Facing Milan's exotic line-up of world stars, our Gazza looked weedy. With Riedle injured, Doll played up front – or would have done if he had been allowed to. As it was, he was regularly forced back into a midfield already occupied by Winter and Gascoigne. Lazio thus had three playmakers with no one to play *to* – except Signori, who was repeatedly caught offside by Milan's robot-like back four. As a result, the three of them kept getting in each other's way. Lazio fought well, but the eventual score – five-three to Milan – made the game sound tighter than it was. At times, Milan's high-speed, one-touch interplay seemed telepathic. And most of it passed Gazza by.

But surely our expectations were absurd. He must be tired. On the morning after the Norway game, Gascoigne had caught a six a.m. flight to Perugia where he was paraded in a money-spinning friendly. From there, on the Friday, it was back to Rome for the pre-match *ritiro*, and then off to the San Siro to be met by Gullit, van Basten, Papin, Baresi and 70,000 baying Milanese. Milan had won last year's championship without losing a game and in the close season had pushed out over twenty million pounds on new players – including thirteen million for the raw Lentini from Torino. AC Milan's owner, the limitlessly rich media mogul Silvio Berlusconi, had worked out that the best way of weakening the opposition was to buy up *all* the talent that was going – no matter that it then languished on his bench. So far this season the team had yet to drop a point. I longed, of course, for Gazza to sparkle in this company, even merely to gain its respect. The word was that two years ago Milan had decided that he was not good enough for them. *Not good enough*? I'd spluttered at the time. It was sad, therefore, to see him so diminished, so peripheral. But surely they too must know that he was knackered.

Three days later, Gascoigne was back in London, for the return match against Tottenham at White Hart Lane. He played for fifty minutes, ineffectually, then took his bows.

At the presentation afterwards, he raised a modest laugh by debagging Sclosa just as the Lazio captain was readying to hoist aloft the so-called Coppa della Capitali. For Spurs fans, it was a melancholy night. We had watched the Norway game with pride. We knew now that Gascoigne was fit again and would probably get fitter. But we also had to acknowledge, for the last time, that he was no longer ours. When he left the field, he saluted the terraces and they saluted him, but there was a weariness, an exasperation even, in the handclaps and the cheers – a sort of 'if you're going, *go*'. As so often, the *Spur* found the words:

> I still can't get used to seeing him in that pale blue Lazio shirt . . . he's like some bird that's chucked you. Your ex is out on the town with a new love, flaunting it, and not giving you a second thought. So you find someone else, and tell yourself you are happy and you're over it. I really thought, I really *really* thought I had got over Gazza.

Il Commento Gastrico

I N THE OLD days, when a British star went to Italy, he disappeared. There would be bulletins from time to time but these would be irregular and mostly scandalous and their import was likely to be reassuring: our favourite would soon be home. In the case of Gascoigne, though, we heard from him each week, on Channel 4's *Gazzetta Italia*, a Saturday morning compilation of Italian soccer news, 'presented by Paul Gascoigne'. And, when possible, the same channel would feature Lazio on their Sunday afternoon 'live match from *Serie A*'. Before we knew it, we were getting to be experts on Italian football: would Juve get their act together this year, had Fiorentina bought too many forwards, would Napoli survive the departure of Maradona to Seville? We knew about Vialli's head-shave, Roberto Baggio's pigtail, Daniel Fonseca's teeth. Channel 4's timing had been perfect. With Des Walker, David Platt and Gazza at three different *Serie A* clubs, there was always a good chance of a Brit slant, and the *Gazzetta* briefing allowed us to talk knowingly of Des's rivalry with Lanna or of Platt's with Andy Moller; it gave us the context and the gossip.

Gascoigne, we heard, was getting £1,000 a week for his

Gazzetta chores, and these were hardly onerous. He appeared briefly at the top of the show, saying something like: 'Hello, I've had a very interesting week. But more about that later. Now *this* . . .' and we would then be handed over to the voice of Kenneth ('They think it's all over!') Wolstenholme, which would lead us through the last week's clips. Then came James Richardson with a somewhat shrill resumé of the Italian soccer press. And then back to Gazza for two minutes of anodyne reflections on 'my week': 'As you can see I had a very tough match this week. The England match was very good but on Sunday people say I looked tired. It wasn't that I looked tired; it was because we were up against a very, very strong team in Milan – one of the best teams in the world.'

In addition, there were Gazza's Golden Goals – 'They have a panel of guys who choose but I am asked my opinion' – and Gazza's prediction of next week's *Serie A* results: 'Ancona versus Parma. This will be a tough match. Zero-zero.' This sequence of the show was so nakedly unauthoritative that after a few weeks it was quietly dropped.

But after a few weeks the 'Gazza factor' was no longer reckoned to be crucial. A *Guardian* survey in December showed that Sunday afternoon Italian soccer was pulling audiences of more than two and a half million, compared with the 600,000 who watched BSkyB's exclusive coverage of all the most important English games. 'Different people will quote different figures to support their case,' said Neil Duncanson, head of sport at Chrysalis TV (the company that produced the Channel 4 coverage), 'but the one I like is the one that says that for the Sunday before last 116,000 homes equipped with BSkyB were in fact watching our programme.'

At Sky, there was a feeling that someone had blundered: Sky had itself once held the rights to the Italian League but had relinquished them in the euphoria of being able to broadcast English premier division games exclusively. The reasoning seems to have been that British fans would never take to the Italians' sterile, defensive style of play. But Sky was not to know that in 1992–93 this style would change – not least because of the new rule prohibiting goalkeepers from handling deliberate back-passes. In the opening weeks of the Italian season, there had been results of three-three, four-nil, seven-three, five-three: figures unthinkable in the heyday of *catenaccio* (or 'bolt', as in 'I bolt the door'). The goals-average in 1992–93, so far, was 3.45 per game compared to 2.27 the year before.

Was it just the back-pass rule that had performed this miracle? Some observers believed that the influx of top foreign players was equally significant. Liam Brady told the *Independent*: 'Time and time again when I was playing there, in the mid-80s, you would just face a wall of ten players. You would get teams going away from home and just camping in their own half. The foreign players who play the game to see who can score most goals have changed the Italian mentality considerably.' It also helped that, under the three-foreigners rule, none of these imported stars could be certain of his place.

Lazio had had one or two goal sprees but had also been on the receiving end – as in the game against Milan. They looked a good team going forward but in defence they had one or two day-dreamers. In this respect, they were a lot like Spurs: when the cockerels go two-up they change into peacocks and all of a sudden it's two-two. Lazio, in the first half-dozen games of the new season, had confirmed their reputation as Italy's draw specialists. Since their promotion to *Serie A* in 1988, they had drawn just over half their games – a record that was beginning to eat at the nerves of their supporters. Last season's anti-Zoff campaign had been revived, and by November the indications were that he was on probation. It was said that the Lazio-Roma derby game on 29 November would seal his fate, one way or the other. A draw in that game would be bearable. After all, Roma were looking good. A defeat, though, would bring down the roof.

Zoff had to hope that Gascoigne would come good before that date. The signs were promising: indeed, the month of November can now be viewed as the purple period of Gazza's first Italian year. The month began with an exhibition game in Spain, against Seville – a match billed as 'the battle of the number 10s – Gazza and Maradona face to face on the world stage for the first time'. The reason for the fixture, from the Spanish point of view, was to help fund Maradona's purchase from Napoli. A large part of his five-million-pound transfer fee was unpaid and overdue. And although Seville fans were unresponsive – only 1,500 turned up to watch the game – the screen-rights had been sold to Italian television.

Maradona's contribution to the game was sparing. He curled a free kick against the bar and delivered one superb overhead cross from a tight angle, and was happy enough to let these two moments serve as his credentials. Gascoigne played for only one half and seemed at first to be aping the Argentinian's haughtily negligent approach. After thirty minutes, though, he stirred himself and scored. A thirty-yard dash took him past three defenders, and two more were on top of him when he shot. The strike was low, angled and unstoppable. Afterwards, Maradona called him 'a great player' and hinted that Gazza might turn out to be his own worthy successor. 'I suppose that was nice of him,' said Gazza, 'But I still remember the hand of God. I tried to kick him for you, Peter [Shilton].'

This patriotic postscript was for Channel 4 consumption and was no doubt aimed at the fans who turned out in force at Wembley a week later for England's World Cup game with Turkey. Turkey, with San Marino, were the punch-bags of England's World Cup group. Before the game, Graham Taylor and others tried to build up the opposition, just in case: after all, were they not managed by the wily Sepp Piontek? Piontek, it was predicted, would have Gascoigne man-marked. It would be up to Paul Ince and Carlton Palmer to clear space for Gascoigne to shine in. As it turned out, he was gifted all the space he needed by the panicky, retreating Turks. And, majestically, he made the most of it. He scored two goals and made one in England's four-nil win. Against Norway his intervention had been critical but brief. In this match he was at his best through-out, superbly dominant in everything he did. His two goals were virtuoso pieces: for the first he skipped between two floundering defenders; for the second he burst on to a lucky bounce in the Turks' area, dummied the goalkeeper, then more or less walked the ball into the net. And it was his elegant flick-on that set Wright free to cross for Shearer's diving header.

England's victory was hailed as comprehensive: by general consent, Gascoigne was reinstated as the nation's saviour. Graham Taylor, for one, could not conceal his gratitude: 'We have been ekeing out results without Gascoigne. I can't remember any player who has influenced a team so much.' For the first time since taking charge of England, he 'felt like a club manager again. There was a nice warm feeling in the dressing-room. A pity we can't play another game next week.' The players also paid tribute to Gascoigne's effect on their morale. 'Just to look at Gazza in the warm-up gives you a lift,' said Lee Dixon, 'Tony Adams winds people up shouting his head off, Stuart Pearce makes sensible points in his quiet way, but Gazza can just stand there and everyone thinks: "Here we go." He doesn't do anything specific or say anything specific – he is what he is.' What the players also admired was Gascoigne's commitment to the team; for all his fame, he had not become 'big-headed'. And they loved his sense of fun. Before the game Carlton Palmer had cut the toes off Gazza's socks: just for a joke, like. Did Gazza mind? Not a bit of it. Next time he'd be looking out for Carlton's shoes. Before returning to Rome, Gazza donated his £3,000 man-of-the-match award to the team 'pool'. 'My mates did a wonderful job,' he said. 'It was a team victory.'

'Please God don't let anything go wrong for this lad,' said Taylor at the post-match press conference.

Like what? he was asked.

'This fellow has got something about him which can still,

if we're not careful, bring him down. You're on edge all of the time with him. He's probably at his most vulnerable now he's back playing. He has time to think about other things, and it could be that people may suggest he gets involved in all sorts of things.'

What sorts of things?

'Other human beings. He enjoys life to the full and might get sidetracked.'

And this was a cue for Taylor to be asked if he could now reveal why he had dropped Gazza for that Ireland game in 1990. His reply was characteristically teasing and obscure:

I can never actually say everything about that decision. I was concerned about his health. It was my first experience of seeing somebody who looked quite glazed at times. Everybody always wants a bit of the boy, but I need him for England. That's the tightrope. The reasons to drop him were not tactical. There were certain incidents before the game. The boy was in a state and I was concerned about his health.

And that was as far as he would go. Which is to say, not very far – and yet too far. Gascoigne, we knew, disliked this kind of managerial speech-making – to the press, behind his back – but he said nothing. The subject would come up again, though, and was clearly at the crux of his relationship with Taylor. Back in Rome, the Lazio-Roma conflict was at hand. On Channel 4, Gascoigne confided that he had never known a build-up so protracted and intense. 'For three months all the fans have been saying "win the derby, win the derby" or "don't lose the derby". For them, it's life or death.' After forty-eight minutes, death seemed the likelier outcome. When Giannini scored for Roma, the Curva Nord broke into chants of 'Dino, go!' and the Roma fans responded with *Serie B! Serie B!* – all this to an accompaniment of smoke-bombs, fireworks, flares, even the odd bonfire here and there. Gazza looked drained and out of touch – rather as in the Milan game that had followed his triumph against Norway. But he had had two weeks to recover from the Turkey match, and for once Zoff decided to let him play the distance. 'In a match like this,' he said later, 'a player like Gascoigne, even when he's struggling, is still always going to make a difference.'

And so it proved, although the miracle came late. With three minutes to go, and with Roma sitting on their one-nil lead, Signori lifted a hopeful free kick into the box. Four players jumped for it, but it was Gascoigne who made contact. A powerful glancing header and Lazio were safe. One-one. It was Gazza's first league goal in Italy. His tearful dance of celebration lasted for two minutes and would have gone on longer if his team-mates had not dragged him back on to the field. He was booked for the delay but didn't notice. For the last seconds of the game he wandered free, muttering to himself, punch-praying with his fists, still choking back the sobs. 'Yes, it was the old waterworks again,' he said afterwards. 'I've never felt pressure like that, not even in the World Cup, because of what would have happened if we'd lost. Ever since I got clumped by that fella in the discothèque I'm still a bit frightened of supporters.' (It so happened that he *was* attacked by fans: three days after the game, Gazza was molested by a gang of nuns. 'I've never had anything like it, nuns, Roma supporters, giving us punches on the arms. I thought nuns were really nice. Incredible. Getting punched by nuns.')

The *Irriducibili* had put on a grateful show when Gazza scored but at the end they were still calling for Zoff's head. When some of the players threw their shirts into the crowd, the shirts were instantly thrown back. Next day, the press was scathing: the game had been a bore, they said, a contest of 'many nerves and little football'. In revenge for this, the Lazio squad announced an indefinite '*silenzio*', a media blackout. In England, though, nobody cared that the game had been no good, nor even that Gascoigne had played badly. It was HAIL CAESAR in the *Mirror* and HE CAME, HE SOARED, HE CONQUERED in the *Sun*. And the tears were, of course, lapped up: 'There they were – those tears of joy that have become his trademark. Yet again it was all too much for a kid who has never really had time to grow up.'

A week later, Gazza scored his second goal for Lazio, against Pescara, and it was one of his best ever – a near-replica of the strike against Seville, but this time the defenders were not playing in a friendly, and the final shot was more spectacular, hit high and hard. It was Gascoigne's last game of 1992. He was substituted near the end with a 'thigh strain'. He then caught 'flu and missed Lazio's next game – a stirring three-one win over Inter Milan. But even in this match Gazza caught the eye: '*Divertendo tutti in tribuna, con scene di esultanza ad ogni gol della Lazio.*' In other words, he really got behind the lads. Or, as he put it: 'I saw the game from a supporter's point of view.'

The Lazio squad was required to report back from the Christmas break on 28 December. Their first game of the

New Year would be against Ancona on 3 January. Gazza would not be playing. The rumours were as usual: a merry Christmas in Dunston had piled on the pounds. He was in need of 'special training' before he would be fit to play. And there were other vexations: while he was away his villa in Rome had been burgled, and in Newcastle his uncle Ian had got into trouble – attacked with a bottle, it was said, by some 'fucking nutter' who had just got out of jail. Uncle Ian would be 'recovering' at Villa Gazza. Gascoigne then had to break training and fly back to England to attend his father, who had fallen seriously ill.

It was 10 January before he was ready to turn out again for Lazio – more than a month since the game against Pescara. By this time the Italian press was offering mid-season breakdowns of '*il Gascoigne Italiano*', his performances in Italy so far, his '*infortuni, spettacoli, gol, botte e lacrime*'. The figures were none too impressive: nine games had been played, and in four of these he had been substituted. Three matches had been missed because of injury or illness or – in this latest case – '*il padre malato*'. Altogether Gascoigne had been on the field for 630 minutes. He had scored two goals (as many, it so happened, as Vialli) and had provided one 'assist'. He had 'procured' one penalty. And the match-by-match analysis revealed that his overall play had been erratic: in most games he had flitted in and out of the action. And he was right to believe, as he did, that the goal against Roma had been vital. Without it, the fans might now be beginning to pull faces, and so too might Dino Zoff. Lazio's official line was cryptic: Gascoigne, they said, was '*importante, ma non indispensabile*'. They were 'disappointed' that he had failed to keep in shape during the mid-season break.

So far, Zoff had not had to resolve his 'three foreigners' dilemma. Both Doll and Riedle had at separate times been injured, and only once or twice had the manager been forced to choose. Injuries can of course be invented, in order to save the face of an excluded star, and this might have been the case with Gascoigne's thigh-strain, or even with the 'flu that kept him on the sidelines against Inter. The Inter game was now regarded as a high point of Lazio's campaign so far, and had been seized on by some critics as a portent: perhaps the presence of Gascoigne, with his special status and his suspect stamina, his '*bizzarrie*', had inhibited the team. Without him, Lazio had seemed faster, fitter, more spontaneous. And this argument was strengthened by Gascoigne's current 'poor condition'. Cragnotti was heard to remark that 'without Gascoigne we had eleven Gascoignes'.

On Channel 4, Gazza replied to the soccer writers who were calling him 'stressed, overweight', not worthy of his place. 'I'd like to see some of these guys, if their father has an operation, if their uncle has a slit throat, your house gets robbed, they take a helluva lot of stuff, then you come back and they expect you to be happy straight away . . . It's just a pity when you stop speaking to people they just go and cause more problems.' It was the familiar plaint: the press tell lies about you so you refuse to speak to them so they tell even bigger lies. What was a chap to do?

In the past, Gazza's most effective answers had been delivered on the field of play. During the first weeks of his comeback he had been fired up, he said, by a determination to 'prove people wrong', and in his two games for England he had surely done just that. Was this defiant fire extinguished now? Was the adrenalin beginning to run low? After his Christmas knees-up in Newcastle, he was now faced with six months of heavy exile, of training twice a day and of lengthy *ritiri* with team-mates who, nice as they were, did not speak Geordie. His days off would be mainly spent behind the walls of his now-burgled Villa Gazza.

The domesticating influence of Sheryl and her children had, he attested, made him more settled and responsible. He had been smartened up. On a shopping trip with Sheryl he had bought '£30,000-worth of designer clothes – in one go' – every bit of it, alas, now nicked, along with a wardrobeful of Sheryl's equally expensive gear. In Rome, his idea of a good time was to watch Postman Pat videos with little Mason and Bianca: 'I get a load of popcorn and bottles of Coke and settle down on the settee. I let the kids stay up so I can see the films.' But even Postman Pat could pall after a time, and so too perhaps could Mason and Bianca, although there was no doubting Gazza's devotion to the kids: 'I have always liked children. I could play with them all day. To Mason I am the only father he has ever known because he was six months old when I met Sheryl. When I am away he'll come to the phone and ask: "Daddy, are you playing football?" It gives me a real thrill to hear his voice.' In England, Colin Kyle, the children's father, had begun legal proceedings to prohibit Mason and Bianca from living abroad. The action was scheduled to be heard in early February.

* * *

With Riedle injured, Gascoigne returned to action against Brescia but was again substituted after a marginal display. The same thing happened a week later in the three-one defeat at Napoli. This time Gazza vehemently claimed that he had taken 'a nasty knock on me hip'. Lazio's next test would be at home against Juventus, which shared with them joint third place in the league. The Juve game was always an event and it was not often that Lazio faced the Turin side on equal terms. David Platt had a knee injury and was out of the Juventus team, but Gascoigne felt certain of his own place: certain enough to invite over a contingent of family and friends, a home from home. On the Friday before the match, though, Zoff told Gascoigne that he was dropped. By all accounts, he took it hard. Some stories have him refusing his reserve-team bib and exiting from the training ground, enraged. Others tell of him drowning his sorrows on the night before the game.

Most of these stories were to be heard, or overheard, in the bar of Rome's Foreign Press Club, where I was entertained by the *Guardian*'s Paddy Agnew, who also covers Italian football for *World Soccer*. Agnew, a Liam Brady fan, was fairly scornful about Gascoigne – not fit to lace the boots of Brady or of Best – and so too were the other journalists I spoke to. A chap from the *European* told of a press conference where he had put it to Gazza that one of his tackles might, perhaps should, have earned him a red card. 'Have you ever played football?' asked Gascoigne.

'Well, no, not really, not . . .'

'Well, fucking shut up then.'

Others weighed in with similar anecdotes, and when I

told them that I was hoping to write a fan's portrait of the star, there was general incredulity. Why bother? Gascoigne, they said, thinks with his feet. But all of them were keen to know what I knew about Sheryl and about the daily routines of Villa Gazza. When I told them that I only knew what I read in the papers, *their* papers, incredulity softened into a sort of pitying contempt. 'If you could get one minute in his kitchen,' said Agnew, 'your story would be written. I mean, does anyone *cook* in that place?'

On Sunday, though, thanks to my contacts, I had access to the Olympico's press box and from where I sat I could see Gascoigne, next to David Platt, looking chirpy and spruced up in his Lazio club blazer. His mates, plus brother Carl and uncle Ian, were in the back row of the VIP area. They looked and no doubt felt conspicuous with their shaved heads, their tattoos, their ready-for-the-business bomber jackets. Surrounded by Italian toffs, they did their best to play it cool, but their cigarettes were kept well out of sight behind their backs, and their refreshments were demurely tucked beneath their seats. There was a blonde girl with them: was this Sheryl or was it Gazza's sister Anne-Marie? In the press box just behind them there was much consultation on this point. Somebody thought he recognized Anne-Marie's husband, a non-skinhead sitting to her left. It must be Anne-Marie. Did Sheryl ever go to Gazza's games?

The match ended in a one-one draw, but Lazio dominated in the second half and would have won if Riedle – back in action and replacing Gascoigne for this game – had not bungled a last-minute chance. Riedle, to everyone's surprise, was emerging as Lazio's 'fourth foreigner': it was he, and not Winter, who had made way when Gazza played, and there were reports that he would soon be transferred. Brought back for the Juventus game, he was too scurrying, too eager; even his famous headwork was awry. The watching Gascoigne knew that his own place in the team was guaranteed for Lazio's next fixture – a mid-week Cup-tie against Torino – because Thomas Doll would be suspended for that game, but in the long term it was Riedle's form that mattered.

In the car-park after the match, Gazza was in jovial mood. If there had not been a *'silenzio'*, he might even have shared a few thoughts with the milling hacks. Lazio was now one of four *Serie A* teams to have announced a boycott of the press, and the scribblers, with three dailies to be filled with soccer-chat, were getting desperate. As it turned out, Gazza saved the day – indeed, he saved the week. Approached by an Italian television crew with a question about being excluded from the team, he grabbed the interviewer's microphone and released into it – a belch: nothing Falstaffian, more a side-of-the-mouth hiccup, but unmistakably non-verbal. The incident was shown that night, at peak time, on one of Italy's most popular shows, and next day the papers had plenty to report.

'Il commento gastrico', *'il rutto in stereofonia'*: Gazza's belch was headline news, and not just in the sports press. In *Il Messagero* and *La Stampa*, there were deepdish editorials on the meaning of Gascoigne's 'pure and spontaneous vulgarity'. What had happened, it was asked, to the manners of the English working class, to Orwell's miners, Kipling's soldiers? Did *they* belch on television? 'The next

116

move must be made by society which cannot permit such lapses of taste.' And this was the view also of a neo-fascist MP Giulio Maceratini (a former member of the Lazio youth team). In parliament, Maceratini demanded an official inquiry into the affair; he wanted 'disciplinary measures . . . a lesson in civility for a champion who seems to ignore the most elementary rules of polite society.' Lazio, clearly embarrassed, tried to calm things down. Zoff admitted that Gazza's 'gesture' had not been at all 'pretty', and Cragnotti said, 'It's all right to do that when we are among ourselves, but not in public when you are wearing the Lazio uniform.' All the same, he said, 'I like Gascoigne very much and I desperately want him to do well.' 'The character,' he said, 'the will to win' was there for all to see. The 'dignity' would surely follow in good time.

In England, the inclination at first was to mock the po-faced Italians. The *Guardian* ran a jokey leader on international belching customs, and the tabloid subeditors made merry: 'Belch Up', 'The Italian Yob'. Brian Glanville, who on a recent visit to Rome had felt the rough edge of Gascoigne's tongue, was pleased that the Italians were now seeing 'the real Gazza': 'Club president Cragnotti is said to feel "betrayed". What a silly fellow. Didn't the penny drop when, first meeting Gazza in his London office, he saw our hero shooting paper pellets from an elastic band? One dropped on Cragnotti's head.' Gascoigne, said Glanville, had the brain of a four-year-old, and it was all to the good that, with his belch, he had broken free 'from the hypocrisy and the smoke-screen which has surrounded him ever since he got to Rome. Free from the conspiracy of silence between Lazio and the Roman press which pictured him as a reformed character, belying the image he brought from England.'

Gascoigne's immediate advisers were divided on the matter of the belch. Jane Nottage, his day-to-day representative in Rome, admitted that it had been 'very unfortunate'. The Italians, she said, were 'always conscious of their image'. Ms Nottage, author of a spicy novel called *The Italians*, had her own problems coping with Gazza's whims and humours, as she had explained to me when I met her in London two months earlier. On that occasion she had been haughtily protective of Gazza-the-property: she told me my face was on the Gazza dartboard because of an article by Brian Glanville in *World Soccer*. Glanville had told Gazza to 'watch out, there's a poet about' and had made me out to be a highbrow sneerer. Nottage said that she might be able to help me with my Gazza studies, perhaps as a co-writer, but we never managed to arrive at an agreement. Her view of Gascoigne, it seemed to me, was rather more *de haut en bas* than mine could ever be. She was not, let's say, a totally committed fan.

On the matter of the belch, Nottage had to tread carefully; she had to stick up for her client without offending the Italians. Mel Stein, based in London, had rather less to lose, and was in any case unresponsive to the Italians' sense of style. Had he not first been seen in Rome wearing a floral beach shirt, shorts and shades, with sandals and brown socks? It was his view that 'the Italians have no sense of humour. It was just a joke. If Paul had done it in England everybody would have laughed.'

But in England the belch-story ran and ran, with mockery of Italian solemnity soon giving way to contemptuous reappraisals of the Gascoigne psyche. Belch-related feature articles appeared: the decline of English manners, the abuse of celebrity, the menace of the 'new Englishman' who was 'increasingly being seen as a brutish and leering figure with little or no right to respect'. This last treatise, by a professor of 'cultural studies' at Lancaster University, was adorned – in the *Daily Mail* – with good-old-days photographs of Stanley Matthews, Biggles, *Brief Encounter* and Phileas Fogg. On the facing page, there was Vinnie Jones, a frame from *Viz*, a *Spitting Image* puppet of Prince Charles and – most prominently – Gazza, in yob mode. A few days later and the gallery of virtuous old-timers would surely have included Bobby Moore. When Moore announced in mid-February that he was suffering from cancer and would shortly die, there were at least two newspaper articles contrasting his gentlemanly ways with the repellent gracelessness of Gazza.

Long before the English had settled into their moralizing plod, the Italians' indignation had burnt out. At the Lazio training ground two days after the belch, Gascoigne had a two-hour confrontation with Cragnotti. There was unconfirmed talk of a £9,000 club fine. Certainly Gazza got a talking-to. He was advised that Cragnotti saw him as 'team leader', as 'one of the crucial components of Lazio's future.' He must therefore 'show maximum commitment, seriousness and concentration.' In the end, his aim must be 'to show us all he knows about football, to show us his technique, but above all to show us the team leader'.

On the following day, Gascoigne recorded his 'my week' spot for *Gazzetta Italia* and asked forgiveness for his indiscretion. His demeanour was sheepish, naughty-boy. The stand at the training ground was filled with English journalists, and every so often he would glance up at it. He knew why some of these newsmen had been drawn to Rome. Rumours were abroad that Sheryl, with the children, had quit Villa Gazza, and that her flight back to England was perhaps connected to the belch and/or to the Villa's recent influx of house guests.

The house guests were in attendance now as Gascoigne said his piece to Channel 4. The group of them made for an odd spectacle: the celebrity in dandyish, bright yellow jacket and checked waistcoat; the lads, beer-bellied, vigilant, in functional T-shirts and jeans. The lads looked like bodyguards, except that now and again one of them would giggle. And what was the star saying to the cameras? 'I'm sorry for me little belch.' Half an hour later, as Gazza was being driven from the ground, his exit was blocked by a small crowd of Lazio *tifosi* – quite a few of them beer-bellied and skin-headed too. They vespa'd to the training ground each day, to watch and wait. There was no need for Gascoigne to apologize to *them*, and he knew it. He signed autographs then rode off, with a lordly wave.

I too was at the gate, the fan from home. I had got chatting with Gazza's brother-in-law, the non-skinhead in his entourage. He was more interested in discussing Oldham Athletic's chances of avoiding relegation than he was in talking about Gascoigne, or Lazio, or even Spurs, but he was amusing on the subject of Italian fans. At training grounds in England, he said, the spectators were mainly 'little kids'. In Italy, they were all teenagers and grown-ups.

On one occasion he had seen a sixty-year-old Italian burst into tears when Gazza looked at him.

And on Thursday night, against Torino in the Cup, he was indeed 'Gascoigne, un Lord, as the Gazzetta dello Sport would dub him on the Friday morning. This game against Torino was his finest hour – or half an hour – in Italy so far. For the first time, his whole repertoire was on display, and the Italians marvelled. And so too did the lads. Every time Gazza pulled one of his breath-taking stunts – a defence-destroying pass, a mesmerizing run, a spot on cross – he would turn to the VIP box and salute his skinhead troops, as if to say: That was for you, for us. And they'd be on their feet, punching the air, no longer conscious of the toffs. The toffs, anyway, were cheering too. Then Gazza would be off again: another pass, another run, another victory salute.

It was, at last, an Italian Gazza-show, more impressive even than his exhibition against Turkey. The Torino back four were not used to being treated with such high disdain, and a quarter-full Olympico was not the same as Wembley. But Gazza once again had things to prove. For four days he and his friends had been held up to ridicule. They had been mocked for their crudity and lectured about 'style'. Very well then, his performance seemed to say: this is my style. When Gazza walked off at half-time, his team-mates lined up to shake his hand.

At that point the score was two-one to Lazio, but it could, should have been five-nil. Gascoigne had set up both of his team's goals and had created several openings that might have been made more of. He himself had been thwarted by an acrobatic save by Marchegiani. And then, just before half-time, an error in the Lazio defence had let Torino in. In the second half, Gazza was spent. He puffed and strained but had nothing left, and Zoff pulled him off with half an hour to go. He left the field, arms held aloft, and the crowd rose to him, respectfully – there were more claps than cheers.

Torino equalized in the last minute when Lazio's goalkeeper, the oft-maligned Fiori, let a soft free kick squirm through his legs, but afterwards the talk was all of Gazza. And one moment in particular stayed in the mind. Halfway through the first half, a high-speed shuffle of the feet had taken him through a ruck of four defenders. It was the shuffle, a kind of feint or jinking quick-step, that captured the Italian imagination. Gazza's manoeuvre, it was said, had a distinguished name – '*il passo doppio*', derived from the 'paso doble' dance-step – and it also had an ancient history. Invented in the 1930s by a Bologna player called Amadeo Bavati, it had over the years often been attempted. Never before tonight, though, had it been executed with the speed and flair of the original. The papers the next day had cartoons and diagrams to show how the move worked, together with photographs of the esteemed Bavati. In 1939, playing for Italy against England, Bavati had employed the '*passo doppio*' to bewilder the Inglese full-back Habgood (sic). And there were columns of awed homage to the reinventive artistry of Gazza:

The '*passo doppio*' of Gascoigne blossomed at the Olympico under a light rain. A ballet improvised and seductive, it caused the pleasure of enchantment to gush forth. Gascoigne on the bathed field achieved something rare and incandescent. This unconstrained lunatic Gascoigne has exhumed an ancient and musical movement which has the rare beauty of a valuable relic. The '*passo doppio*' is of the history of football. It is as precious as the miniature lettering of an antique manuscript . . . And it adds beauty to the chiaroscuro of the situation that this pearl has an heretic for a father . . . On Thursday Paul, in a game of pure elegance, has redeemed his recent pig-like belch, worthy of Gargantua. He has restored the magic of a tapestry. With beauty he has confounded the critics. He has given the game the dignity of the dance and he has transformed the field into a drumskin.

Well, that's roughly what it said. And whatever we may think of its author, one Claudio Gregori, he's a world away from Harry Harris.

Did Gascoigne *know* that he had so redeemed himself? If so, he made short work of his halo. Two weeks later, in Turin for the return leg of the Cup-tie, he was in the news again. A distinguished *Il Messagero* journalist called Maurizio Saticchioli approached him in a hotel lobby: 'I went up to him and said "Good evening",' said Saticchioli. 'He got up, signalled for silence, lifted his leg and broke wind. He tried to fob off the blame for his performance on the kit man, who was sitting next to him. But the kit man denied it and everyone knew it was Gascoigne. Then he started laughing. Everyone else was extremely embarrassed. This Gazza is clearly a real gentleman.' On the plane back to

Rome, after the *Il Messagero* story had appeared, Gascoigne berated the reporter for his breach of confidence: 'Fuck off,' he is said to have said. 'I fart whenever I want to.'

Portly Again?

'ENGLISH FOOTBALL'S most precocious and precious talent is evaporating into the skies over Italy like the fading flares of a half-spent Roman candle. Somebody, somewhere, has to be brave enough and rich enough to say, Gazza Come Home.'

This was the *Sun* on 18 February, the day after England's World Cup match with San Marino. England had won the game six-nil, but this was not reckoned to be much of a result. Had not Norway recently put ten past these postmen and bus-drivers, these *Serie B* rejects? For days the English press had been predicting a double-figure massacre, with bags of goals for Gazza. On the night, though, England laboured, and four of the six goals arrived late in the game. By then the crowd had remembered the words of 'Wot a Load of Rubbish' and had taken to booing John Barnes every time he touched the ball. Poor Barnes, just back after a bad injury, had played as he always plays for England, abstractedly, but he had made one of the goals and had done some nice things now and then. Why the yob nastiness? Some observers believed that the crowd's exasperation had more to do with Gascoigne than with Barnes. Gazza had struggled from the start. He had been jittery, ill-tempered, slow. After Norway and Turkey, this match was meant to be a Gazza-fest, but the star of the show looked as if he wished he wasn't there. The hype-crazed fans had been let down – but how could they boo Gazza?

In fact, Gascoigne was by no means the feeblest England man on view. Nobody played well and the full backs, Dixon and Dorigo, probably had most to answer for; with no forwards running at them they should have been romping down the wings – getting to the byline, getting crosses in. Actually they did romp down the wings, but the crosses kept landing in the crowd behind the goal. Still, that was the way it was with Dixon and Dorigo: what did anyone expect? At one point, after Dorigo had been grounded with concussion, the England trainer told Graham Taylor: 'Tony's hurt – he doesn't know who he is.' To which Taylor is supposed to have replied: 'Tell him he's Ray Wilson.' With Gascoigne the difficulty was that he was 'not himself', and most of the post-match analysis centred on this issue: what had gone wrong with our messiah?

Taylor, needless to say, was both gnomic and expansive. The lad was 'having a struggle with himself'. He was unfit, overweight. He had perhaps peaked in the games against Norway and Turkey: 'In his mind he had won the battle to prove us all wrong and get back on the pitch.' Since Turkey, 'his fitness has slipped away'. If it continued to slip, 'Crikey, we may not be able to get fifteen minutes out of him.' So were the Italians to blame for not having kept Gascoigne up to scratch? On this, Taylor put on his diplomatic face; his relations with Lazio were excellent. What was it then; who *was* to blame? 'He is a very emotional boy. He seems unhappy with himself and within himself. His eating habits

126

go with the moods. When he's unhappy, he finds solace that way.'

There was plenty to get stuck into here. 'Unhappiness' surely had to do with what the hacks, off-duty, referred to as 'the great divorce'. Since leaving Italy in January, Sheryl had been holed up in Hertfordshire, saying nothing, but her mother had been telling the press plenty. Sheryl's life in Italy, it seemed, had been a lonely yawn. The girl 'hated football'; she missed the discos and the bright lights, '*la dolce vita*' of Dobbs Weir. When Gascoigne was off for days on end, in *ritiro* with the team, she spent her evenings on the telephone to mother. In Rome she could not go shopping without the paparazzi on her heels; she had no social life; she could not speak the language. And she found it hard to cope with Gazza's frequent house guests – especially his mum, Carol. Even so, she still loved him, and there was no doubt that he loved her, although snaps taken of the pair in restaurants and airports always showed Sheryl looking cross and Gazza looking contrite and bewildered. When Jane Nottage later told all to the *Sunday Mirror*, this impression was confirmed: Sheryl, said Nottage, was the stronger of the two and something of a shrew. 'He seems totally obsessed by this woman. She obviously has something he needs. When he's with Sheryl, he gets uptight and nervy. They quarrel constantly when you're with them: it's like the Battle of Waterloo. Paul is a sweetie when he's on his own. It's pathetic. Paul's family are his rock, his stability. I think he should look very carefully at his relationships, and ask if he is really happy.'

For Gascoigne, the week before the San Marino game had

127

been packed with Sheryl-incident. Her husband, Colin Kyle, had won his court injunction: if she wanted custody of Mason and Bianca, she would have to live in England. Colin, we read, was a bankrupt and therefore unable to make trips to Rome. Although Sheryl had unsuccessfully appealed against the ruling – there was a court hearing in Cambridge on the day before the Fart – pressmen privately figured that she rather welcomed its constraints. From now on, she would visit Rome alone, stay in a hotel and enjoy city-nights with Paul: no more Villa Gazza, no Carol, no Five-Bellies, no four-day *ritiri*. For Gazza, of course, all this meant no more Postman Pat.

Sheryl's first visit to Rome since the 'divorce' had been a week before the San Marino game and had ended chaotically. She and Gazza were in a restaurant, staging a lucrative reunion-with-Sheryl photo-shoot, when some lensmen from a rival newspaper happened to appear. Fisticuffs ensued. Five photographers ended up in jail, and Sheryl headed – 'grim-faced' – for the airport. Sheryl was now perpetually, almost officially, 'grim-faced'. Gascoigne, it was thought, had had further words with her before the Wembley match. And in between these meetings, if Graham Taylor's hints had been correctly understood, the player's head was in the fridge.

In Italy, when Taylor's comments were decoded, there was understandable resentment. It had never been Dino Zoff's policy to push Gascoigne hard during his first year with Lazio: the 'pain barrier' could wait. He wanted to bring him along gently, both as a player who had been seriously injured and as a personality whose culture-shock would necessarily be difficult to manage. Zoff had several times said that only next year – 1993–94 – would he expect the 'real Gascoigne' to emerge. Hence the substitutions, the rest periods, the tolerant approach to Gazza's conduct off the field. And Cragnotti, although more impetuous and star-struck than the coach, took a similarly patient line: 'Of course you cannot go around belching and farting, but I honestly don't think that these last two incidents were the real Gazza. I think he's an intelligent man who likes to wind people up. Paul is very important to us and it is up to the club to help him as much as we can. He can stay as he is – like a clown – and that clowning could complete his image as a great player. I expect to see the real Gazza at the end of this season, and eventually the Lazio team will form around him.'

Graham Taylor could not afford to be patient. He wanted the real Gazza now. As a club manager, Taylor had been affably paternalistic: the players who worked for him were *his*. He knew when to cuddle them, he claimed, and when to kick their backsides. Not so with England. In the international set-up, 'his' players actually belonged to Alex Ferguson, or Terry Venables, or Dino Zoff. Even John Barnes, his one-time Watford favourite, had other masters now. And with Gascoigne, Taylor's control was most painfully tenuous. He could not get at Zoff through the English Football Association, as he could with any recalci-trant club manager in England. Indeed he had to be careful not to tread on the Italians' toes. In Italy, players really are owned by their clubs, and why should Lazio trouble them-selves with England's World Cup woes?

So far Lazio's interests had roughly coincided with Taylor's. Each wanted Gascoigne revived as a world figure: Taylor for obvious reasons and Lazio because much of the club's income came from exhibition games, starring the 'new Maradona'. But should there be a falling-out, Taylor had more to lose than Zoff. And the San Marino game neatly illustrated the underlying differences between the two of them. Gascoigne was clearly not fit to play a ninety-minute international. He had been involved in four matches during the eleven days leading up to San Marino, and off the field he'd been having a rough time. At Wembley, if Dino Zoff had been in charge, Gazza would have been pulled off after sixty minutes, if not long before. Taylor kept him on. But why? If he had replaced him, he said, 'it would have destroyed the lad.' Kindly considerations of this sort had not influenced Taylor's treatment of Lineker in Sweden. Was the manager afraid? Afraid of the crowd reaction, the press, of Gascoigne's wrath – which, on that night, was surely on the boil? Or was he simply waiting and hoping, as we were, that something miraculous would happen, and that tomorrow's headlines would speak not of a ponderous, heavy-weather victory over sub-standard opposition, but of a Gazza-inspired goal-blitz? Managers are also fans: they fantasize. And they can have their ugly moods. From Gascoigne, Taylor needed a Norway and a Turkey *every* time, just as we all did. With San Marino it was a fit of fan-exasperation that led the manager to inflate an off-day into an existential crisis. But what of the burden on Gascoigne, the burden of not knowing *how* to 'turn it on?' After Taylor's provocative post-match soliloquy, Lawrie McMenemy did his best to head off the 'Gazza Come Home' school of psychotherapy. He suggested that perhaps

Gazza's unhappiness was more to do with his art than with his life: 'His unhappiness comes from the frustration of a person with such great natural ability who is wondering why he is unable to produce it as much as he would like. It is nothing other than that. It is not a personal problem, it is not about living in Italy. It is about a lad who is searching for the answers himself and wanting to sort it all out.'

McMenemy's hunch was that Gascoigne was better off in Italy than he would have been had he stayed on in England. And, all things considered, we bereft Gazzamanes were beginning to agree. In England, there was an essential hostility to Gazza: a class fear, a culture-dread. Here he could be *placed*: on the terraces or on the rampage, down the pub or up before the beak. If we were to meet him, we'd be ill at ease – both awed and condescending, with the condescension somehow managing to win the day. When Gazza speaks on television, the English – or most of them – mock his *Auf Wiedersehen Pet* accent and his all-over-the-place syntax. But in Italy, most people think he's speaking proper *Inglese*, or that his dialect is interestingly regional. In England the belch was seen as no more than you'd expect from such as he. In Italy, it was thought to be out of line but idiosyncratic. And the Italians were not in the least disconcerted by other, to us off-putting, aspects of his physicality: his huggings and kissings of colleagues, his patting of bald heads, even his sniffing of opponents' armpits. They saw him as generously tactile: we saw him as over-the-top, gross. In England, all but one or two of Gazza's mentors wanted him to change, to grow up, to become more like David Platt. In Italy, as Cragnotti testified, they regarded the nuttiness as an important aspect of his gift – and the gift was what mattered above all. 'In many ways,' said Jane Nottage, 'Paul's character fits into the mentality of the Italian people very well. He has a genial side and a dark, self-destructive side, which is very Roman.'

The conventional wisdom about English players in Italy is that success comes only to those who 'learn the language'. Repeatedly, on television and in the press, Linguaphone veterans like Ray Wilkins and Liam Brady painted a grim picture of what life for Gazza would be like should he fail to make an effort on this front. We heard that he was taking Italian lessons twice a week, but few really expected him to persevere, or to get much beyond the basics. As Mel Stein once pointed out, he was not a lessons sort of guy. With his Lazio team-mates he rubbed along, but comically, by mono-syllable and mime – and the comedy, by all accounts, was helpful. Not speaking the lingo, Gazza was free to be pure clown. According to Ms Nottage, 'The rest of the team might speak Geordie before Paul speaks Italian.' Most Lazio players could now swear in fluent Tyneside.

Watching the team training, I found it hard to detect rivalries or tensions. The Italian players seem mightily amused by Gascoigne and are both indulgent and protective – parent-like, in fact. And he is, of course, remorselessly bubbly and prankish, and always on the move: one moment teaching the Italians how to make authentic British V-signs, the next demonstrating his kung fu expertise. And in five-a-side games he does more than his fair share of Euro-yelling. All in all, the atmosphere seems boyish, a bit silly, but OK.

But tensions and rivalries were there. When, at the end of February, Lazio lifted their media embargo, both Riedle and Doll had lots to say. In their view, Gascoigne was getting preferential treatment. Why was it always one of the two Germans who got dropped? Riedle said: 'We are just fed up that he does what he likes and is still guaranteed a game every Sunday.' And when Doll was left out for the 28 February fixture against Genoa, he too made his displeasure known: he resented Zoff's last-minute methods of selection; he never knew until the Saturday who would be in the team next day. Gascoigne, of course, always knew.

Throughout February and March, 'Gazza Come Home' stories continued to appear in England. There was a possessiveness in these stories: Look what they're doing to our lad. But there was also a rebuke: Look what our lad has done to them. Blackburn Rovers were said to have offered Lazio four million pounds for Gazza. In Italy such rumours were dismissed and Mel Stein said that we could take his word for it that Gascoigne would see out his five-year contract. On the field, Gazza continued to perform fitfully and was usually substituted after an hour's play. He seemed to see the sense of Lazio's gradualist policy, and to know that his stamina was not yet what it was.

Against Genoa on 28 February, though, his removal from the arena was on the orders of the referee. The oft-predicted red card had finally been shown. But the surprise here was that most Italian observers were surprised. The particular offence was relatively minor – the bad-tempered elbowing of a too-adhesive marker – but even this was thought to be untypical, or 'out of character'. Since his arrival in Italy, Gascoigne had built up a reputation for good-humoured resilience in the face of enemy attack. There had been moments of petulance – he had to date chalked up two bookings – but on the whole he had been a model of

restraint: he made a point of shaking hands with opponents who had fouled him, or whom he had fouled, and for smiling matily at referees when they scolded him.

There was an amusing moment in Lazio's home game against Sampdoria. Gazza, irked by a decision, ran to the referee as if to register a protest. The ref reached into his pocket and took out not a yellow card but a much smaller object, which he handed to Gascoigne. It turned out to be chewing gum. Gazza popped the gift into his mouth and ran off, twinkling. And the referee looked happy too. I was not certain that I approved of this new Gazza, spreader of sunshine: it all seemed too calculated, too self-consciously compliant, and – although of course we thoroughly abhorred foul play and the questioning of referees' decisions – I worried that by blunting the player's Northern belligerence these genial Mediterraneans might also be blunting his resolve. With Gazza, the balance had to be just right.

After Gascoigne got his marching orders against Genoa, he ran around shaking hands with his opponents – including the one he had tangled with (Bartolozzi; he who chopped Gazza down on his Lazio debut). What was our rude boy up to *now*? Was he *apologizing* for his own wrongful dismissal? Or was he secretly taking the piss? Gascoigne's 'outrage turned to a smile', said the *Gazzetta dello Sport*. 'Boyish, perhaps, but Gascoigne is his own man – no aloof aristocrat but prepared to give himself to his public and make us laugh, or at least smile. What more can we ask in these hard days?'

Gazza's hand-shaking act paid off. He was suspended for one match instead of the anticipated two. And this meant that he was well-rested for Lazio's home game against Milan, on 14 March. For Gascoigne, this meeting had assumed a large significance. The last time he had faced up to the Italian champions, he had been cruelly over-shadowed, overawed. His pretensions to world status had been called into question: Gascoigne looks good against the likes of Turkey but put him in with the big boys and he is instantly dwarfed. This was the whisper back in October, and it hurt. Gazza, we hoped, would be in one of his 'something to prove' moods.

And for Lazio as a team there was more at stake in this encounter than mere points. Four days earlier, Roma had beaten the champions two-nil: in the Cup, admittedly, and there was a second leg to come, but even so. Milan had gone forty games without defeat, and it had been Lazio's despised rivals who had been the first to cut them down. Lazio fans, who might in other circumstances have settled for a re-spectable defeat, now wanted blood: whatever AS Roma could do, Lazio could do better, or – at worst – just as well. And it so happened, anyway, that Lazio might never get a better chance of conquering Milan: the red-and-blacks were fielding a much-weakened team – none of their three Dutchmen would be playing, and their goalkeeper, Rossi, had a patched-up shoulder. Against Roma, as Lazio kept pointing out, Milan had had a seventeen-year-old between the posts.

In the event, Lazio drew with Milan two-two, but it could have been much worse. They had come back from two-nil down and had controlled the play for most of the second half. And Gascoigne it was who pulled the strings. After a tentative first quarter of an hour, he gradually emerged as the game's dominating presence, with Baresi and co looking unusually anxious whenever he was on the ball. In the October fixture, the midfield was like a war zone, and Milan were the gung-ho aggressors. At the Olympico, two-one up and intent on salvaging two points, they backed off and relied on their offside trap to nullify the dash of Fuser and Signori. Gascoigne, lying deep, had room from which he could direct the forward play. His through-balls to the front men had to be varied and accurate, and so they were – all the more so as his confidence grew into a mild cockiness. Before long he was making a few forward runs himself. For the record, he scored one goal (a tap-in from two yards) and assisted in two or three glorious near-misses. But this was no triumphalist occasion. It was an almost cerebral affair, a matter more of self-respect, of 'How good am I, really?' than of wishing to prove others wrong. Dino Zoff called it 'Paul's best game, considering the quality of the opposition.'

Gazza did not repeat the triumph in the 1992–93 season. Indeed, the Milan game turned out to be the climax of his year. For myself, I am inclined to wish that the season *had* ended that day. Two weeks later, playing for England against Turkey in Izmir, Gascoigne was marked out of the game and only a smart headed goal in England's two-nil win prevented a re-run of Graham Taylor's San Marino speech. With Lazio, he had little more success. In the April derby against Roma – a neurotic nil-nil draw – he was peculiarly disengaged, even before a knee injury forced his withdrawal from the game. A *knee* injury! At first it did look bad – Gazza suddenly pulled up in mid-stride and clutched at his scar, the scar that by now I'd half-forgotten. In the end, a muscle strain was diagnosed, but for the few days leading up to Gazza's next game – England's Wembley World Cup match against Holland – the old anxieties resurfaced. I had occasion to reflect on just how far Gascoigne had travelled since he had first taken the field against Tottenham in Rome. On that night I had winced every time anyone came near him. Now, when some bloodthirsty Turk spent ninety minutes hacking at his legs, I found myself wondering if he still had the power, the verve, to cope with a man-marker.

On the day before the Holland match, Ruud Gullit – via the *Daily Mirror* – told Gazza that 'You'll *never* be the Same Again': he, Gullit, had taken a year-and-a-half to come back from his knee operations and the worst part had been having to accept, when he was fit again, that it was 'not possible to do again what you have done before.' In his prime, before the injuries, he used to make fifty runs to deep positions; nowadays he could manage only twenty. 'But it's important that when you do it those twenty times, they are done well.' Gazza should follow his example: accept his limitations, alter his style of play and settle into a new, mature phase of his career. Gullit was now thirty-one: Gazza had just turned twenty-six. Was this a pre-match 'psych'?

At Wembley on 28 April, the Gullit-Gascoigne confrontation turned out to be a flop. Gazza, elbowed in the face by Wouters, was taken off in the first half with a broken cheekbone, and Ruud was eventually substituted: a tactical move that resulted in Holland's equalizing goal. Gazza, and England, had looked good in the first half, but the loss of a home point meant that their end-of-season away fixtures against Poland and Norway were no longer games that England could afford to lose.

Gascoigne would be needed for those games. On 1 May, he had an operation 'to strengthen a depressed fracture of the cheekbone'. He would be out of action for perhaps three weeks. England were scheduled to face Poland on 29 May, Norway on 2 June. With luck Gazza would make it, or – in the *Sun*'s words – NORWAY WILL OP STOP ME. The player seemed to welcome the respite: he was at once off to Eurodisney with Sheryl and the kids. And when he reappeared on 16 May, playing for Lazio against Ancona, he wore a funfair look: a yellow carbon fibre mask had been prescribed, as protection for his damaged cheek. Gazza was delighted with this new accessory: in a way, it was what he'd always wanted. 'I told the lads I was the Phantom of the Opera,' he said. 'I don't think they'd ever heard of it. They have now – and so has all of Italy.' In a five-nil win that took Lazio to within two points of qualifying for the UEFA Cup, he was in clownish mood, but deadly. He set up two of the five goals. The first of these, tapped in by Riedle, was the climax of an extraordinary Gazza run. He took off from his own half, ran fifty yards and left four Ancona defenders on the floor, outpaced and looking dizzy. He could have scored himself but, at the last second, he rolled the ball across goal to his German rival: a magnanimous touch for which he later took full credit. 'Beauty in a Mask' was the Italian press response. Two days later, a burglar broke into the Lazio training ground and made off with just one item: Gazza's now-celebrated facewear. The police were not sure that the matter ought to be pursued: it was a crime, they said, 'for love of Gascoigne'.

'I think I'll wear it all the time,' said Gazza, when a replacement was procured, and he took the mask with him to Poland and to Norway. We all know what happened next: a lucky draw against the Poles and in Oslo a defeat that had the press shrieking for Graham Taylor's resignation. These results meant that England would probably not qualify for the 1994 World Cup finals in America. The hacks' vacation plans may have to be revised. One paper featured a pile of horse-manure on its back page. Gascoigne, mask and all, had looked weary, out of sorts. After the Poland match, Taylor singled him out for special criticism. The whole team had performed like 'headless chickens', but it was Gascoigne's performance that had annoyed Taylor most of all. It was the San Marino script, but read with more vehemence, more rancour. It was all very well, he said, for Gascoigne to claim that he trained hard in Italy; 'It's a matter of how you feed and refuel yourself between training sessions. This is something Paul has to come to terms with.'

'Refuel'? Did this mean food, or drink, or – dare the word be mentioned – drugs? Taylor would not be drawn, and Gascoigne made light of the whole business. Drugs could be ruled out: had not Gazza recently spoken out against Caniggia, the AS Roma player now serving a hefty suspension for cocaine abuse? Well yes, he had, sort of. He'd said: 'It's a shame on sport, but it's his life, he can do what he wants. If he gets caught there are problems. I don't know what cocaine does for you before a game but he has been scoring some good goals lately.' The food we knew about: the Fat Boy pigged out when under stress, and sometimes when not under stress – he liked pizza, pasta, mozzarella cheese, steak, chips and *see*-food ('That's when I eat everything I see'). It had to be the drink. And here Gazza confessed that he did have a problem: *what* should he be drinking, beer or wine? 'The doctor at Lazio told me I should be drinking wine because it would be good for me. When I did, he had one look at me and said, You'd better go back on the beer.' He promised that he would put things right against Norway. And we believed him: he usually came through when it mattered. In that disastrous game, though, he looked even more sluggish than he did against the Poles. And much the same could be said of the whole team. The jubilant Norwegian coach declared: 'They gave up in the last fifteen minutes. I've never seen an England team do that before.'

Gazza went back to Rome, disgraced. From there, he tried to be generous to Taylor: 'I felt sorry for him. We all let him down.' But he was clearly riled that, once again, he had been singled out. 'Don't forget,' he said, 'there's eleven players on the field and I cannot – these people expect me to do it week in, week out, and I cannot.' As usual, he didn't need the press (or, he might have said, the manager) to lecture him: 'I know exactly where I'm going wrong and what I've got to do to put it right.' He had been accused of over-eating, over-drinking – well, sometimes he played *better* when he was 'a little overweight'. This was a new one, but worth pondering: if it was true that Gascoigne spent the day before the Norway match in a sauna, trying to 'get fit', perhaps the whole matter of his podginess ought to be re-thought. He was looking forward, he said tauntingly, to a close season of 'pizzas and beer'.

Gazza made little or no contribution to Lazio's last game of the season – a four-one thrashing at Juventus – but nobody seemed to mind. Lazio had qualified for the UEFA Cup for the first time in seventeen years. All in all, it was reckoned that 1992–93 – and Gazza – had gone well: next year would be the year. Meanwhile England, in a close season 'Americas Cup', were being hammered by the USA. For Gascoigne there was news of other hammerings. Mel Stein, indicted for fraud in a Louisiana court, and now under threat of extradition, had placed himself in psychiatric care. Jane Nottage, Gazza's on-the-spot Rome gofer, had turned traitor: fired by Gascoigne in the wake of some Sheryl-related rumpus, Nottage was selling her *Paul Gascoigne – the Inside Story* to the Sunday press – a story in which Gazza would be portrayed as a bulimic booze-hound, with Sheryl as his devil-woman aide. (When Nottage's memoir appeared in book form in September, there was more in it about money and Nottage's personal grievances than there was about Gascoigne the player, and even the low gossip seemed to have been padded out, but there was one 'revelation' I will particularly treasure. It turns out that Gazza *is a poet*! Or, as Nottage puts it, he now and again savours 'the joys of dabbling in poetry-writing'. Before the Lazio-Roma derby, he penned the following, in Nottage's note-pad:

> *Blue is the colour*
> *Lazio is the name*
> *I am the other*
> *Football is the game*

> *Now never mind the league*
> *Or the bastard cup*
> *Because when we play the derby*
> *We will fuck them up.*

And at Spurs, Terry Venables – the manager who 'took me from a boy to a good class player' – had mysteriously been sacked. Spurs had an option to buy Gazza back if Lazio should ever wish to sell. With Venables gone, there was 'no way' that Gascoigne would return.

He did return, but briefly, at the beginning of this season, in a competition for something called the Makita Trophy. Two teams from England – Spurs and Chelsea – were up against Ajax of Amsterdam and Lazio, in a four-match knockout. For the Spurs fan, this two-day tournament was an ordeal of divided or stretched loyalties. We didn't know which way to turn. Terry Venables had been banned from White Hart Lane by Alan Sugar, but sitting in his place was Ossie Ardiles, another of our all-time greats. And Glenn Hoddle was now a player-manager for Chelsea. Then there was Gazza, in Lazio's light blue. What we should have wanted was for Tottenham to crush Lazio and for Chelsea to be crushed by Ajax who in turn Tottenham would crush. We should have been yelling for Anderton, Barmby and Sheringham to show the door to these oldies and exiles, these ex-Spurs.

In our hearts, we yearned for something else. At least, we snowy-haired ones did. We yearned to see Hoddle up against Gazza – not up against, but on the same field, just once. We wanted to see them marvelling, gaping at each other's gifts. We wanted them to swap shirts at the end, like Moore and Pele. Or better still, they could throw away those peculiar blue vests they wore and call for new ones – white ones, with a cockerel on the chest. And then the two of them might do a lap of honour, to the strains perhaps of 'Ossie's going to Wembley/His knees have gone all trembly.' Do you remember 1981? And, since it was party-time, perhaps a few others could join in. Ardiles *and* Venables, for sure, with Stevie Perryman in tow. And Steve Archibald, maybe, and Crooks, and Dave Mackay and Jimmy Greaves and Blanchflower, and even the now-dead John White, the one they used to call 'The Ghost'.

The 'nothing-tournament' in fact ended with Chelsea beating us four-nil and with Hoddle masterminding our humiliation. At the end we had to listen to Chelsea fans chorusing Glenn's name – at White Hart Lane. And we also had to listen to Gazza getting booed. He took a dive, the yobbos thought, to win a penalty for Lazio.

But still, it wasn't a *bad* day. Gascoigne scored a brilliant goal, albeit against Spurs. And there was even talk afterwards of Glenn being 'recalled to the England team', with an admiring, fully fit, sober and sensible, mad and mischievous Paul Gascoigne at his side, and with Venables as manager. Just to get us through the next two games, you understand, the Poland and the Holland, just to put us back where we belong.

Lazio: The Beginning of the End

W E LIVE IN dreams, we soccer fans, and after a time we learn how to hoist ourselves from one dream to the next: from Jimmy Greaves to Glenn Hoddle to Paul Gascoigne. With Greaves and Hoddle, my dream plan had been foiled. Greaves did not win the World Cup for us in '66; Hoddle was not the star of Spain in '82. In 1990, though, Gascoigne very nearly got it right – nearly enough, anyway for me to devise for him a sure-fire fantasy career curve: 1994 would be his year, his crowning triumph. In 1990, Gazza was twenty-three; in four years' time, I prophesied, he would be at his peak and ready for world conquest.

Then came the knee, the fear that he was finished, the comeback. And then the Turkey game at Wembley, the *passo doppio* in Rome. The dream was just about still dreamable. It did not occur to me that England might not reach the finals. Even after the away defeat by Norway, I was telling myself that we would make it, that the gods would surely not pass up a chance to see Gazza doing the business in LA. And once we had qualified, the whole shape of things would change. From somewhere we would get a decent team – a team good enough to assist Gascoigne to his date with destiny.

The run in, as I imagined it, would be leisurely but sure of purpose. As from 14 October 1993, when we were scheduled to beat the Dutch in Rotterdam, all the way through to mid-July when we would face, say, Italy or, better still, the Hun in, say, the semi-finals, we Gazza fans would be able to sit back, enjoy the build up, count the days. According to this script, Gazza would arrive at the World Cup in terrific shape, fresh from a resoundingly successful second year in Italy. Lazio, thanks to him, would have won the UEFA Cup, run Milan a close second in the League and done the double over Roma. Gazza's mood would be bubbly but resolute: no fuck-offs, no farting out of turn. He might even have given Disneyland a miss. And then the dream action would begin.

Not much to ask, you'd think. Our script, to be honest, did not even insist that England capture the World Cup. We may be *pleine de rêves*, but we're not nuts. We would have settled for half a dozen workmanlike performances with, of course, Gazza at centre-stage each time. Of him we would have expected just one or two astounding moments of world class. Otherwise, it would have been sufficient just to be there, to have *him* there – and to know afterwards what happened when he finally took on the best.

Soon enough we learned that 'what happened' was not going to happen – not in 1994. And there were those who believed that Gazza himself should take some of the blame. Booked in the three-nil win over Poland, he was automatically barred from playing against Holland. If he *had* played in Rotterdam, would we have won? The dream script says we would.

Certainly Gazza did not blame himself for getting booked. As he saw it, the Poles needled him non-stop, right from the start. There were no Turin-tears this time. Indeed the prospect of suspension seemed to fire him up. Within minutes of his booking, he was elbowing Adamczuk in the face; a bit later, he kicked the ball at a recumbent Pole. He could easily have been sent off. He also scored the best goal of the game. 'I just hope I didn't let anyone down,' he said afterwards. He hoped too that he would be able to join the lads in Rotterdam, to cheer them on, to cheer them up.

As it turned out, Lazio refused to let him make the trip, and that was that: we lost two-nil and we were out. As good as out. There was still one game to play, against San Marino in November. But this, everyone agreed, would be a farce. If we were to thrash San Marino seven-nil and if Holland lost to Poland in their final game, we might still have a chance. Some hope.

Meanwhile, the arithmetic that mattered was already sinking in at the FA. Failure to qualify was going to cost thirty-five million pounds or thereabouts. To establish the exact figure would mean commissioning an 'impact study' which would itself cost £50,000. Sponsors were in furious retreat, travel agents were being swamped with cancellations. And who could estimate the hidden toll: the national psyche locked into a year-long depression, our pride of country sapped? Within days of the Rotterdam defeat, state-of-the-nation jeremiads began appearing in the press. 'Why are we no good at anything?' became the general cry. England's cricketers had just been trounced by the Australians; our tennis players had undergone their annual Wimbledon wipe-out. And now this, this Rotterdamnation, as the *Observer* chose to call it. For this someone must pay.

Graham Taylor was the obvious first casualty. He bowed

out after the San Marino formalities were tidied up (we did score seven goals but, as a farewell jest, we also let one in – during the first minute of the game; Holland, of course, took care of Poland and went through). And other scape-goats were lined up: Des Walker, Carlton Palmer, David Seaman; the referee who didn't send off Koeman; Charles Hughes, the FA's long-ball strategist; the 'grass roots' that had thwarted the flowering of our national 'technique'.

In these hit-lists, Gazza was mentioned now and then, but listlessly – of him what more was there to say? His punish-ment, it seemed, would be gradual and unspoken. A leakage of charisma had begun. He was no longer the magical unknown, the one who would eventually deliver. Since 1990, whatever his setbacks and follies, there had always been the big 'what if?' What if Gascoigne got healthy/sane/grown-up in time for World Cup '94? After Rotterdam, 'what if?' became 'what now?' And in some quarters the answer was: who cares?

Well, we did. And to prove it we could show you our *new* blueprint. In 1996, England would host the European Championship – or Nations Cup. In that year Gascoigne would still be in his twenties – twenty-nine, to be precise. There would be a new manager, a new-ish team, and no hassle about qualifying. It was not the World Cup but it would be the next best thing – and it would happen here, in close-up.

You *have* to be a fan to think like this. In domestic football we learned long ago that self-delusion is the key. When our team gets knocked out of the FA Cup, we pretend that we are glad: 'now we can concentrate on the League.' When we get relegated we are grateful: 'now we can rebuild with no pressure.' When we run out of money, we say 'phew – at last we can develop a youth policy.' And so it is with England, and with Gascoigne. If we could make it through to August, if we could get this Mickey Mouse American World Cup behind us, we'd be fine.

Of course, we needed Gascoigne to be with us, on our wave-length. And here there was the shadow of a doubt. We are never sure that our football heroes suffer as we do. We hear talk of them joking around in the team bus after a five-nil defeat. When interviewed after some terminal setback, they seem more interested in hair gel than in the black weeks that lie ahead. And they tend to talk in TV-speak, mechanically upbeat. At best, one of them will admit to feeling 'gutted' but that's not enough. We want from these felled champions an unequivocal, spot-on depiction of our own distress. Hence the success of Gazza's tears. But was he crying in 1993? On the morning after England's match with San Marino, he failed to show up for a recording of his regular Channel 4 TV spot. David Platt was hastily re-cruited to replace him. Gazza, we learned, had been allowed to attend the last rites in San Marino and had doubtless been 'fueling around' with the lads afterwards. No one had seen him since.

This sounded promising. Perhaps his post-match *accidie* was on a par with ours. We knew, though, that he had other reasons to be glum. His second season in Italy had got off to a bad start. He had returned from the summer break a stone-and-a-half overweight. Dino Zoff had been 'amazed' by his condition. Amazed and angry. And Dino was not noticeably cheered when Gazza added to his poundage by fixing himself up with a shoulder-length hair extension. The new locks were modelled on Roberto Baggio's but the effect was more like Benny Hill in drag. After one or two risible outings on the field, Gazza's hair-piece was abandoned. It had been a good laugh, he reckoned, but Lazio seemed less amused than it might have been a year earlier.

In September and October, Gascoigne made four appearances for Lazio, and was substituted each time. Three days after his non-involvement in Rotterdam, he succumbed to the first of a series of small injuries that would keep him out of action until mid-December. First there was a muscle strain, then a long bout of tendinitis. In between there was some new bother with his knee. In late October, he was sent back to London for a consultation with John Browett. After an uneasy wait, he was given the all-clear: he would not, it was revealed, 'require an operation'. An *operation*? What did this mean? Were these muscle strains more than they seemed? Or were they, as claimed, offshoots of the Italians' training methods which seemingly involved 'more stretching' than Gascoigne had been accustomed to in England. David Platt, we remembered, had once said something to this effect, and there was a period when he, too, was forever falling victim to small aches and strains. With Gazza, though, there was always this undercurrent of alarm, this fear that, on the matter of his knee, we had never been given the whole story.

Lazio's statements about Gascoigne's serial indispositions were becoming frostier and more evasive by the week. Dino Zoff had taken to shaking his head in mock-bafflement whenever the subject was brought up: it was all a mystery to him. And the *Guardian*'s Paddy Agnew thought he could detect the beginnings of a 'campaign of disinformation' on the part of Lazio's press people. He recalled that when Juventus tired of Ian Rush, the club saw to it that the press was kept supplied with damaging items of club gossip: how Rush had written off two diesel cars by filling them with petrol, how he was always getting lost, how Michael Laudrup could not be bothered to translate for him, and so on. The idea was to project Rush as a dumb-bell and a misfit. By the time he left, no one could remember why Juventus had bought him in the first place.

And now, according to Agnew, the same thing was happening to Gascoigne. A year earlier, his antics had been reported smilingly. When he hid the trainer's car or turned up naked for a five-a-side, these pranks were seen as components of his genius. Now they were reported testily or with a yawn. 'The problem with Gascoigne,' said Agnew, 'is that, although no Lazio official will say so and the club president Sergio Cragnotti and coach Zoff are careful what they say, the word is that patience with Gascoigne is running low.' And Gazza himself had heard as much, it seemed: 'If Lazio *are* getting the hump about me, they'll just have to get the hump because I cannot help these injuries. I've come through the thigh. I've come through the tendon, I can't joke about it any more.'

This was early December 1993. In that month, Lazio was in an especially humpy mood – and not just about Gascoigne. The club's president, Cragnotti, was being investigated by the Milan magistrates for alleged involvement in the Edimont fraud scandal, and was under house arrest. 'The guy who runs the club has been banged up,' said Gazza on TV, as he listed the club's woes. Lazio had been knocked out of the UEFA Cup and the Italian Cup and was now drifting towards the wrong end of the League. Dino Zoff was again reckoned to be on the skids. Some reports had him mulling over an offer from Bayern Munich; others had him heading for the dole. 'It Rains on the Wet,' said the *Corriere dello Sport*, as Lazio crashed to yet another League defeat.

The signing of the Croatian Alen Boksic from Marseilles – for eight million pounds – was viewed as the club's last bid to salvage something from this, its 'breakthrough season'. And it was seen too as confirmation of all the rumours about Gazza: the Englishman would soon be on his way. Gascoigne's appearances so far had cost Lazio £400 a minute, according to one paper.

In England a restaurateur called Gino Santin announced that 'Gascoigne is for sale' and that he, Santin, would 'act for Lazio. I have their blessing that if I get someone interested in buying him, then I can bring the two parties together for talks.' Lazio, when questioned, claimed never to have heard of Santin. And Gazza also knew nothing of this 'Santini, Sabatini or whatever his name is'. He had evidently missed the two British TV programmes in September which had explored Terry Venables's financial goings on at Spurs: in each of these programmes Santin was named as one of the architects of Gascoigne's transfer to Lazio. He was said to have pocketed a 'bung' of some £200,000 for his good offices. He had denied this and would shortly be giving evidence to the Premier League's inquiry into Tottenham's finances.

In spite of all the denials, one or two English clubs did show an interest in buying Gascoigne. Howard Wilkinson of Leeds was one of these, which led David Lacey to observe that bringing Gascoigne to Elland Road would be 'as bizarre as Arthur Miller marrying Marilyn Monroe'. Blackburn and Liverpool were also named as possible bidders but these stories were obvious space-fillers – or so we Spurs fans hoped when the *Mirror* ran a 'Gazza for Arsenal' back page. Unfeelingly, the *Mirror*'s art department had rigged him out in a red shirt, white sleeves, the lot. Another implausible report, in *Football Monthly*, predicted that Gascoigne would be transferred to Milan in part exchange for Papin.

VULTURES HOVER OVER GAZZA'S LAST STAND was one headline on the day before Lazio's game against Juventus on 12 December. Gascoigne was fit at last and had been picked. Boksic would play up front and Gazza would pull the strings from deep midfield. 'I will enjoy feeding on Gazza's passes,' Boksic said. The combination worked. Lazio defeated Juventus three-one and Gazza scored. So too did Boksic. And Gazza lasted the full ninety minutes: indeed, his goal came in the final minute of the game. Best of all, he was not in the least tentative. The old cockiness was there for all to see, and after the match there was general agreement that he had comfortably upstaged Roberto Baggio who was about to be voted Europe's Player of the Year.

After this triumph, there was no more talk of Gazza-for-Leeds, even when, soon after Christmas, he reported back to Italy with a new injury – this time a mysterious groin strain. He had done it, he said, climbing out of bed, and the tabloids were quick to grasp the innuendo. In Italy there was also talk of 'Gazza's crazy Christmas'. And there were accusations that the injury was faked: Gascoigne, it was said, wanted an excuse to spend New Year with Sheryl and the kids. A week later, though, he was recovered, fit for action, and a new rumour started up: that Gazza *had* faked the groin strain, not for Sheryl's sake but as a self-parodying jape. The papers *expected* him to report back for training in bad shape, so here he was — not overweight, as usual, but saucily groin-strained. Gazza: post-modern prankster? Well, why not?

Postscript

I T IS NOW August 1998, a month after the World Cup in which Gascoigne played no part. A Middlesbrough player now, he faces a new season knowing that, for most observers, he has become – officially – a has-been. His name does not appear in a 22-man squad named by Glenn Hoddle for a 'get-together' in preparation for England's forthcoming European Championship match with Sweden. Every other player who was left out of Hoddle's final World Cup squad has been recalled, we note. We also note that Gascoigne's omission has sparked little or no comment in the press. There would have been more response had he been picked.

How did this come about? Five years ago, Graham Taylor dithered about picking Gascoigne, but nowadays the England team boss is a former player notorious for having been underrated by the England management. When Hoddle succeeded Terry Venables, we Gazza fans were convinced that he would back our hero all the way, bring out the best in him, and so on. And at first it seemed as if this was indeed Glenn's view. Early on he made it clear that he appreciated Gazza's soccer gifts and that these gifts were what he'd focus on. The other stuff, the Gazza stuff, would pass him by. Thus, we who had admired the pair of them – Hoddle and Gascoigne – could sit back and await some magical fulfilment. Hoddle, through Gascoigne, would perhaps be able to relive some of his own thwarted soccer dreams. The World Cup of 1998 held the promise of apotheosis.

Well, we all know what happened, and Gascoigne is now 31. Four years ago, when my original Gazza narrative concluded, he was getting on for 27. Ahead of him lay Euro '96 and then France '98. The best was yet to come. Did we really believe this, even then? Wasn't the whole drift of Gazza's story a drift towards some calamitous come-uppance, some terrible bringing-down-to-earth? Or had the bringing-down already happened – in 1991, with his Cup Final leg break? Had *that* been the low point in my narrative – the low point from which our hero would re-emerge, triumphant? But then again, perhaps this hero was never really meant to be heroic? Maybe there was some-thing in his personality that ran counter to the fantasies his soccer gifts induced? Was Gazza actually 'ill-fated'?

Midway through the 1993/4 season, where my story left him, Gascoigne's bosses at Lazio were beginning to ask themselves some similarly awkward questions. Although Gazza now and then came up with brilliant 'cameo' perfor-mances, he was forever getting booked or injured. He had returned from his Christmas break with a mysterious groin strain, and manager Dino Zoff, although not pleased, had tried to play it down: 'A player of his class is always useful, even if he is not in the best condition'. But then other strains and knocks kept cropping up: picked to play in a January fixture against Sampdoria, Gascoigne cracked a rib after fifty brilliantly effective minutes and was taken off. And this became the pattern: short, wonderful appearances and then goodbye. And when he was not injured, he was suspended, or about to be suspended. And Lazio, although high up in the *Serie A* table, always seemed likely to become unstuck. After a 4–0 defeat by Foggia, club president Sergio Cragnotti declared that Zoff's team 'does not have the winning mentality'. Rumour had it that Foggia's coach, Zdenek Zeman, was being lined up as Zoff's replacement, and Gazza was not helping Dino's cuase: on top of his injuries and bookings, he was in trouble off the field. On January 29th, he was arrested by the police for beating up a Rome photographer. Cragnotti, once again, was not amused.

Back in England, the good news for Gazza was that Terry Venables had been named as the new national team coach, and was coming to the rescue of his best-loved soccer son. Within days of his appointment, Terry flew to Rome to check on Gazza's form. And he liked what he saw. On February 14th, Venables watched Lazio demolish Cagliari 4–0 at the Olympic Stadium and, as if to welcome his new boss, Gascoigne put on a brilliant show. After eighty-nine minutes of restrained and thoughtful midfield play, he scored with a superb banana-shaped free kick. To celebrate, Gascoigne did a Tarzanesque swing on the Cagliari cross-bar, 'playfully' kicked the Lazio team bench, and then topped the performance by striking a ludicrous Chris Eubank statue pose, chin up, arm muscles flexed. As he left the field, he aimed a double thumbs-up in Venables' direction.

On the following day, Venables and Gascoigne held a joint press conference in Rome, all smiles and sturdy resolution. 'I have missed him', said Venables, 'and how

POSTSCRIPT

he has matured!' And Gazza responded with near-gratitude: 'I would like to think I'm touching now the standards and fitness of 1990. Maybe there's ten to twenty per cent more to come. But my game here has changed. I'm happier now. I feel comfortable for the first time being watched by an English manager – with Graham Taylor I always felt I had something to prove.' He felt 'ashamed', he said, that England would not be competing in the 1994 World Cup finals. Venables, in reply, praised Gascoigne for having 'settled down' so well in Italy, even though the Cagliari game had marked only his third ninety minutes in twelve starts during the current season.

It was a cosy double-act and yet we somehow felt uneasy: such chirpiness must surely presage trouble. And sure enough it did: two weeks later, in Lazio's derby game with Rome, Gazza was taken off midway through the first half, suffering from 'rib and wrist injuries'. 'I couldn't breathe,' he said. Three days after that though he was playing for England against Denmark. Admittedly, he played a 'quiet' game but his Lazio bosses were surprised that he had been able to turn out at all. Was he playing for Venables or was he playing for Dino Zoff? On his return to Italy, Zoff expelled him from a training session for 'not trying', and Gazza threw a tearful 'nervous fit'. A few days later, he expelled himself: after ten minutes at the training ground, he claimed to have developed a 'pain in the side'. As a result of this new injury, he was left out of the team that beat Napoli 3–1. Worse still, he failed to show up at the stadium on match day. Cragnotti was wearily displeased: 'It is clear', he said, 'that someone who plays one week and not the next three is no use for us. I would like to give Gascoigne a telling off but to do that I have to find him first'. Later, he added: 'He is uncontrollable at the moment. I have invested a lot of money, and this is an investment that should be respected.'

Gascogine's response to Cragnotti's scoldings was more spectacular than surely either of them would have wished. On April 7, two weeks after the club president's statement, Gazza lunged into a training-ground tackle on Alessandro Nesta (then a Lazio youth player) and ended up writhing on the ground. He had fractured his right shin in two places, a complicated break. 'I'm finished', Gazza wept, as he waited for the ambulance. Later that same day, he was flown back to England to be seen by John Browett, the surgeon who had attended him in 1991. 'Bad luck seems to follow him wherever he goes', commented Len Lazarus, but was it just bad luck? After all, Gazza had been playing in a five-a-side game against Lazio's juniors – a pretty trifling encounter. Why had he so violently thrown himself into the fray? Had he been 'wound up' by the disapproval of Zoff and Cragnotti? Had he been squabbling with Sheryl? What was it that had made him try too hard?

Whatever the reason, Gascoigne was going to be out of football for at least six months, perhaps a year: another bout of surgery (metal rods and pins would have to be inserted in his leg) followed by months of gruelling physiotherapy. Before the injury, English clubs had been listening in on Gazza's disagreements with Lazio and some tentative approaches had been made by Blackburn and Newcastle. It was even rumoured that Gascoigne had provoked the disagreements in order to encourage such approaches. Now everything had changed: GAZZA – THE END headlines began sprouting in the tabloids, along with various obituary-style analyses of his unfortunate career. Gascoigne was said to have been 'jinxed' or 'cursed'. 'The devil has hijacked the talents made in heaven', said the *Sun*. He had been brought low, it was said, by 'frailties in his temperament'; 'even when he was airborne he was carried on the flimsiest of wings.'

In Italy too there were doleful summaries of Gazza's Italian adventure – an adventure which, everyone seemed to believe, must now be over. Andrea Galdi, football correspondent of *La Repubblica*, publicly thanked Gascoigne for having brought some laughter into 'the dull world of Italian football', and wistfully recalled his most famous misdemeanours: the belch, the punch-ups, the Sheryl spats, even the 'extra kilograms' he routinely brought back from his holidays. Gazza, she said, may not have lived up to expectations as a player, but no other footballer in Italy could rival 'his impact on the crowds':

How they love it when he waves to them at the Stadio Olimpico, mad with enthusiasm. The people who lock their avid gaze on him when he is playing. The people who carry his picture on their shirts, with the words 'C'mon Gazza'. The people who wait for him outside Lazio's training ground at Maestrelli to shake his hand, to get an autograph, to say to him 'Grazie, Gascoigne'. The people who cried along with him when the local derby with Roma was drawn after he had equalised with his most important goal. The people who yesterday hurried to the hospital where he was recovering after his latest misfortune, just to let him know that they were there. The people who sent telegrams to Lazio. In this, Gascoigne has been triumphant. And what does it matter if he has not earned millions in endorsements? In Italy, Gazza was expected to be a front cover personality and a money-making machine. In fact he has not been. He has not made records, he has endorsed practically nothing, but he has involved and excited the *tifosi* and not just those at Lazio. Gascoigne, who did not go to Eton, is a son of the same working class which has inspired great books and great films. He has won a place of his own, and has been acclaimed escpecially for his 'differentness'. In the real world of Italy today, where the image and rapport with the mass media is so important, where the gods of football have fame and money, Gascoigne is also a spontaneous person – difficult and awkward but appealingly natural, with his impishness and his tears.

Terry Venables, asked if this new injury marked the end of Gascoigne's footballing career, said: 'Absolutely not'.

As it transpired, Gascoigne was out of football for a year, from April 1994 until March 1995. During this year off Venables made sure that his favourite player continued to be 'involved in the England set-up'. He invited Gascoigne along to the F.A. training camp at Bisham Abbey and in various public statements made it clear that he could hardly wait for Gazza to be back in action. He praised the player's 'dedication', his 'disciplined' commitment to recovery. 'The tough times', said Terry, 'are when he is sitting at home and out of contact with people. If he can get his mind right, he will have years ahead of him.' Gascoigne, for his part, was grateful for the chance, at Bisham Abbey, to fool around again with his old England mates. Seemingly, they were more tuned into his sense of humour than most of his Italian mates had been. First of all, though, 'I just have to get back to playing again', he said. Since Christmas 1990 Gascoigne had made only 46 League appearances, in England and in Italy, many of them incomplete, and he had played 10 times for England. 'I feel I have missed three and a half years of my career', he said, 'But I am only 27. I still have time, though not as much as when I was first injured.' In the same interview, he hinted that – whatever happened – he would almost certainly be leaving Italy.

During his year off Gazza had sustained his tabloid prominence by granting interviews which in the past he might have shied away from. Two of these turned out to be sensational. In July, 1994, not long after his accident, he provided the *News of the World* with a four-page 'amazing confession' on the subject of his relationship with Sheryl. For two years, he said, he had been in the habit of beating up his girl-friend whenever, as he saw it, she had showed signs of not loving him enough. He had pulled Sheryl's hair; he'd grabbed her by the arms and shaken her. There had been one or two tackles from behind: 'I kicked her legs'. Yellow-card offences, some might think, but Gazza was blubbingly contrite: 'I've let Sheryl and the kids down', 'I was so stupid', 'I've said I'm sorry to her dad', and so on. All in all, an embarrassing outburst, and thoroughly gratuitous, so far as we could tell. Why, 'out of the blue', had Gascoigne telephoned the *News of the World*'s Rebekah Wade and summoned her to his room in a Bedfordshire health farm where 'between huge, heart-rending sobs and gulps of mineral water, he bared his soul as never before'? The confession, we noted, coincided with the final stages of the '94 World Cup. Even in soccerland, Gazza was a forgotten figure. None of the TV panels had called upon his expertise and the papers had lately been filled with stories about Maradona – another 'tragically flawed soccer genius'. Was Gazza feeling just a bit left out? If so, his intervention was horribly mistimed. On the very day that Gazza bared his soul, the Colombian, Escobar, had been shot dead: for scoring an own goal, so it seemed. Compared to this, Gascoigne's whimperings seemed extra-infantile.

A few months later, though, he was once again in confessional mood. Appearing (at his own request) on a TV show chaired by Danny Baker, he added a few footnotes to the Sheryl tale. The two of them were 'finished' now, he said; and this in spite of several attempts at a reconciliation. 'There is not a relationship any more. We got caught in this love thing.' The real cause of the bust-up was, he said, 'with me not being mature enough'. As if to prove the point, he went on to itemise a few of his neuroses. He could not sleep, he said, unless he had 'the telly and the lights on'. He got frightened when he was alone in the dark he always felt alone: 'I worry about things I shouldn't worry about. I just think about the future and worry.'

He also described his strange tidiness-compulsion. 'I'm giving away my secrets now, but all the towels in my home have got to be level (when piled on a rack). That's terrible, isn't it? I put a towel down and if it's a bit out of shape I tell myself "Don't worry about it. Go to the pub and forget it." So I would lock the door but still go on about the towel all the time. I'd be 200 yards up the road and think "No, go back and sort it out". I'd run back, open the door, and put the towel straight. It was the same when I bought my first house. Everything had to be new and couldn't be touched. I'd hate to invite friends around because they made a mess – even my mum and dad. I'd be panicking if anything got touched or moved.' Odd stuff indeed from a jester who got a kick out of pissing on his team-mates in the shower, or from preparing cat-shit burgers for his friend Five-Bellies.

Gazza's come-back date, according to Lazio, would be April 6, 1995 – almost exactly a year since his leg break. And sure enough, on that date, he lasted a full ninety minutes against Reggiana, with Terry Venables watching from the stand. Gazza had shaved his head and got his weight down (by 2 stones) to around 11½st., his ideal playing weight. In the actual game he did very little but he looked nimble and alert, and the crowd cheered his every touch. Venables called his performance 'quite remarkable'. He could envisage a new role for Gazza in the England team: a role more canny and withheld. Zdenek Zeman, Lazio's new coach (Zoff had been moved upstairs) was less enthusiastic. 'It seems to me', said Zeman, 'that Gascoigne has entertained journalists an awful lot but not the spectators who pay to see games every Sunday. His performance on the field is the only thing that counts for me.' In the Roma-Lazio derby on April 14, Gascoigne was brought on for the last fifteen minutes of the game, with Lazio leading 2–0. Two weeks later, against Cagliari, he was again used as a substitute, this time for half an hour. In neither game did he contribute much. Indeed, so poor was his performance against Cagliari that Zeman afterwards announced: 'Gascoigne can do no more for this club. He cannot be our saviour' He was 'pretty sure', he said, that Gazza would soon be back in England.

News of Gascoigne's possible availability set off a small storm of 'enquiries' from back home. Newcastle, Everton, Leeds, Queen's Park Rangers and Middlesbrough were named as some of the front-runners. The most active and convincing interest, though, was said to be from Glasgow Rangers: according to rumour, Rangers had already come in with an offer. Over the next few weeks other English clubs got mentioned – notably Aston Villa and Chelsea – and it was said that Terry Venables was keen that Gazza should perform in the English Premiership. In fact, Lazio had not yet confirmed that Gazza was for sale. This confirmation came, though, on May 2nd: Cragotti announced that he was considering various bids, all of them from Britain. 'Paul must find himself', he said, 'as a man and as a player, and will do it only by returning home.'

Three days later Gazza joined the England squad at Burnham Beeches in Buckinghamshire, where Venables was preparing his players for a summer tournament, the Umbro Cup, which would involve matches against Japan, Sweden and Brazil. He seemed determined that Gazza would feature in at least some of the forthcoming action, even though he had scarcely played since his return from injury. All talk of turning-points was brushed aside. 'Paul always seems to be at a critical stage of his career, ever since I have known him', Terry said. 'It is a bit of an unknown situation but we all know what he is capable of. I know Paul. He is highly patriotic: to play for England is very important to him.' Gazza himself said that he felt 'like a young kid again. People have written me off but, if I can stay injury-free, I hope I can prove to them – and to myself – that I can be a good player again'. He did concede, though, that he would have to play more shrewdly: 'I will have to use my head more when going into tackles. A couple of times I have been injured from wanting it too much.'

In the event, Venables used Gascoigne sparingly throughout the Umbro tournament, bringing him off the bench in the later stages of each game. It was against Sweden, in a 3–3 draw, that Gazza made his most telling contributions: a free kick from which Platt headed in and an elbow in the face of Sweden's Magnus Erlingmark. Erlingmark's nose was broken and Gazza afterwards was 'absolutely gutted. I didn't mean to do it'.

On the opening day of the tournament, Gascoigne had announced that he would indeed be joining Glasgow Rangers for the start of the 95/96 season. 'It's Rangers for me', he said, on a quick visit to Glasgow for a 'social night' with his reassuringly avuncular new manager, Walter Smith. The transfer fee would be £4.3 million, the wages just over £15000 per week, plus a cut of the inevitable 'merchandising'. The news was greeted with some puzzlement. Why had no English clubs pushed harder for his signature? Was this a wise move – for Rangers, for England, or for Gazza? Rangers, after all, were paying a record fee (and record wages) for a player who had been out of football for a year. Walter Smith was perhaps over-desperate for his team to make an impression on the European Champions League, a competition in which Rangers failed dismally each year; but would Gascoigne, an Italian reject, really make a crucial difference?

As for Gazza himself, surely this Rangers move was a step downwards. Week in, week out, he would be up against pushover opposition: he would shine, no doubt, but would he not slow down, become complacent? There was also, it was said, a risk of further injury: the Scottish League would have plenty to offer in the way of mistimed tackles and retributive hard men. And what about the private life? Glasgow was not Rome or London. Gascoigne would be the centre of attention in a city almost pathologically obsessed with soccer. How would he handle the Rangers-Celtic thing, the sectarian intensities, and so on? When the news of his Rangers transfer became public, Glasgow bookmakers were offering odds on Gascoigne getting sent off in his very first Old Firm match.

Gascoigne of Glasgow Rangers arrived in Scotland on July 11, 1995 and at Ibrox he was greeted by a thousand gaping fans. Nobody, it seemed, had quite believed that he would actually show up, but here he was, and sporting a ghastly new peroxide hair-do. He was feeling 'very fit', he said, and couldn't wait to line up for Rangers' first pre-season friendly – against Brondby in Denmark. Scottish football, he declared, would prove more challenging than critics in England were predicting. He was 'fed up with people putting down Scottish football'. It was his intention, he pledged, to 'talk and play it up'.

Rangers' tour of Denmark was notable for yet another Gascoigne elbow job. What was it about Scandinavians? The Rangers fans no doubt were glad to learn that their new hero was no cissy. For them, the real action would begin at Ibrox, with a triangular pre-season tournament featuring Sampdoria, Tottenham and Steua Bucharest. Gazza's debut, against Bucharest, was full of promise. He linked up well with Brian Laudrup and for the first fifteen minutes of the game the two of them were dazzling. With a new horde of *tifosi* to enrapture, Gascoigne ran through his repertoire of party tricks. Just before half-time, though, he made sure that the game would not be remembered for his soccer brilliance. First he aimed a kick at a Romanian midfielder who had fouled him and shortly afterwards he celebrated a tap-in goal by miming the flute-playing of a Protestant bandsman. This moment of play-acting was not widely noticed at the time but photographs of Gazza the Orangeman were all over the next day's papers. For a just-arrived Englishman to announce his 'tribal affiliations' in this way was generally reviled as 'stupidly ill-judged'. Gazza was, of course, apologetic. He had had no idea what the gesture signified. His team-mate, Ian Ferguson, had told him that this was Rangers' 'traditional' ritual for goal celebrations. He had simply been trying to 'fit in': 'When I scored the goal, I've done the old action', Gascoigne later said. 'After that it was just unbelievable: people just wanted to kill us. They were just going barmy. One guy stopped his car and said: "Gazza, you just watch what you're doing up here. Be careful, mate." So I went: "Cheers, mate". And he went: "'Cos I'll slash your effing throat". The training session didn't go too well that day. I was running around and you could see the pap out of my underpants all day.'

Gascoigne had had a similar response a few days earlier when Sherly – with whom he had yet again been 'reconciled' – announced that she was pregnant. Gazza 'really, really shit me pants', when told the news he later testified. 'I took it in a bad way. Instead of, you know, putting my arms around her and saying "Great, that's what we always wanted", I really really panicked. I think she was worried, definitely, that I might turn nasty again – in reaction to the baby.' And sure enough, she was: Gazza was 'thrown out' of her Bedfordshire residence and Sheryl was all over the papers, vowing that this time she really meant it. Gazza struck back, though, within days: limousines full of red roses and protestations of late-found paternal zeal. Earlier in the year, after one of their bust-ups, he had bought Sheryl a '£3000 boob job' and in return she had agreed to take him back. This time she was less susceptible. In numerous tabloid articles she was said to be 'just not interested any more' – even when Gazza, repeatedly, proposed a speedy marriage. 'Friends' of the couple were quoted as saying 'Paul has got some work to do before Sheryl even thinks about seeing him again – let alone walking up the aisle.'

Sheryl aside, Gascoigne's first season in Glasgow must be counted a success. More consistently than at any time since 90/91, he came up with stretches of match-turning brilliance: the tight control, the surging runs, the dead-ball wizardly – the whole repertoire was on display, game after game. The fans, as always, loved him but the management, it sometimes seemed, was not so sure. There were the usual bookings and sendings-off and some of Gazza's best performances were against relatively feeble opposition. Most importantly, though, he did nothing much to improve Rangers' standing in European competition. His sending off, for 'dissent', against Borussia Dortmund was seen by the club bosses as a dismal postscript to yet another botched campaign in Europe. Rangers ended up at the bottom of their group.

In addition to the Dortmund episode, Gascoigne was regularly in conflict with officialdom in Scotland: once for a head-butt (against the chest of an Aberdeen defender), once for pinching an opponent's bottom, once for showing a red card to the referee. (The ref had dropped the card and Gazza picked it up, flourished it in the ref's face and was then mightily downcast when, in reply, the humourless official flourished it at him.) The Aberdeen incident was reported to the police and for a time there was a fear that Gazza might follow Duncan Ferguson to Glasgow's Barlinnie jail. In the end the 'case' – for assault – was quietly dropped.

The Rangers' fans, of course, delighted in such scandals and such impudence, and many of them felt that Gascoigne was getting unfairly singled out by referees. From the supporters' point of view, this player had delivered when it mattered – against Celtic (who failed to beat Rangers in six meetings) and in the season's climactic, championship-clinching defeat of Aberdeen, a game in which Gascoigne scored a hat trick. This match, in April 1996, was the crowning triumph of a splendid season: a season that saw Gazza voted Scottish Footballer of the Year, both by the sports' writers and by his fellow players. In May, reflecting on his season's achievements, Gazza was full of praise for Walter Smith and for the Rangers coaching staff. Smith, he revealed, was not always as kindly as he seemed. On one occasion, several months ago, he had dropped Gazza from the team. This, said Gazza, 'gave me the kick up the backside that I needed. Walter said that I was injured but in fact I was dropped. He saved my life.' On another – or was it actually the same? – occasion Gascoigne confessed to Smith that he, Gazza, had had a drink a few hours before some vital game. As a result, Smith had not spoken to his player for two weeks. This too had had a salutary impact, we were told.

In spite of all this upbeat talk, Gazza often told the

English press that he was not happy with his life in Glasgow. He lived in a chalet in the grounds of the Cameron House Hotel on Loch Lomond, about thirty miles from Glasgow. The idea had been that he would find some peace there and do lots of fishing. As it turned out, he found the solitude oppressive. Sheryl refused to join him, and for most of the time his only companion was Five-Bellies. The pair of them spent hours in the hotel brasserie and between meals were often to be seen speedboating on the loch. But there was a tabloid reporter behind every bush and, although Gazza often yearned for the big city, he was determined not to be caught with his pants down in some Glasgow night-club. As always, he was at his most content when cavorting with his soccer team-mates – on the training ground or in the dressing room, and especially in the wake of a new on-field triumph. He was as prankish as ever. 'Never get changed next to him' said Stuart McCall, 'He'll cut the feet off your socks or steal your trousers'. Some of his team-mates (Brian Laudrup, in particular) found some of these japes hard to take, but on the whole the Rangers' lads warmed to him: irritating but lovable, seemed to be the verdict, as with every other team he played for.

At Rangers, the management encouraged off-field camaraderie and turned a blind eye to most of the drinking that went with it. From time to time, according to one Gazza interview, the players got together for a two-day piss-up in a luxury hotel – a sort of conference, or bonding break, as it was no doubt called in Rangers' annual accounts. It was during one of these away-days that Sheryl – in February 1996 – gave birth to little Regan, Gazza's son. Gazza did not make it to her bedside. He was, well, indisposed – well indisposed. Once more, when the story broke, Gazza was full of tabloid shame. 'I don't know why I do these things', he said in a television interview, shaking his head with what seemed like genuine bewilderment. He was then shown changing Regan's nappies and proudly pointing out the infant's 'willy'. Again, the pride seemed thoroughly authentic – but bewilderment still lingered. Can you imagine it? he seemed to say, a mini-Gazza, a Gazza more juvenile than the original! Sheryl, we soon learned, was much displeased by Gascoigne's absence from the labour ward but had decided to go easy on him for Regan's sake. There was talk of the couple buying a house in Scotland but nothing came of this. Gazza the new father continued to commute from Loch Lomond to Hoddesdon, in Herts.

The summer of 1996, the summer of Euro '96, was, looking back, the pinnacle of Gascoigne's soccer life, the high point we had long been hoping for. Pre-tournament, there had been the usual grumbling from pundits who believed him to be past it, or near-past it. He had, they said, dazzled to deceive in Scotland's mediocre League. And, of course, there was a dash of scandal too. As a preparation for Euro '96, Terry Venables decided to take his squad on a tour of China and Hong Kong. In soccer terms, the tour went fairly well – and presumably produced a decent profit too. Gascoigne's performances were much praised for their 'maturity'. Not so mature, though, were his antics in Hong Kong, where he and some of his teammates took themselves to a night club and got plastered. One of the night's party games required each of the revellers to sit in a so-called 'dentist's chair' and have drink poured down his throat. A glazed-looking Gazza, drink in hand and shirt in shreds, was the star of numerous front page photographs next day. Was this the way for our lads to get ready for the nation's biggest soccer test since 1966?

Worse, though, was to follow. On the flight home, the team's aircraft suffered internal damage – a smashed TV screen, broken arm-rests – and once again Gascoigne was fingered as the principal destroyer: after all, it was his birthday. DISGRACE FOOL GAZZA said the *Sun*, and all the other papers followed suit. Although Gazza's team-mates protested that they too had been carousing, the press insisted on heaping all the blame on Gascoigne. Even supposedly in-the-know sports page pundits were depressingly eager to call for Gascoigne's head: to suggest, indeed, that Terry Venables dismiss him from the squad. 'England must sling out Paul Gascoigne on his ear-ring', wrote Jeff Powell in the *Daily Mail*. 'They must devise a way to play without this playboy relic.'

Venables, it need hardly be said, took no notice. And a couple of weeks later none of the critics wished he had. After a quiet start, England went all the way to the semi-final of Euro'96 – via a stunning 4–1 against, yes, Holland – but they would not have got beyond the group had it not been for Gazza's wondrous strike against the Scots. David Seaman had stopped a Scotland penalty; the ball moved from Seaman to Anderton and then, at speed, to Gascoigne, who had Colin Hendry barring his advance. In full stride, Gascoigne chipped the ball over Hendry with his left foot and then volleyed it past Gorman with his right. It was one of his best-ever passes, and he had passed it to *himself*! The goal celebration was meant as a rebuke to the Jeff Powells: Gascoigne slid to the floor face upward, both arms spread, and his chortling team-mates gathered round to pour pretend-booze down his throat. A tawdry spectacle but who could say that he had not earned himself a touch of tawdriness. The goal had been, well, beautifully crafted.

And this is more than could be said for Gazza himself when, in an ivory, gold-embroidered frock-coat and blazingly rebleached crew cut, he limousined to Hanbury Manor Hotel in Hertfordshire for his post-tournament wedding to Sheryl, a wedding stage-managed (for a fee of £150,000) by *Hello!* magazine. Sheryl, four-figure boobs assertively on show, was togged out, we were told, in 200 metres of tulle adorned by 30,000 beads. Gazza had forgone his stag night, at Sheryl's insistence, and was in sober and respectful mode – at least until *Hello!* had got its pix. The chosen music was 'Unchained Melody' and 'Can't Help Loving that Man of Mine', and the guest list included team-mates McManaman, Redknapp and Seaman, a handful of Scots (Ally McCoist and Darren Jackson) plus Venables, Glenn Roeder and Bryan Robson, father figure from the past. Sheryl's family was of course in evidence, positioned on the *Hello!* group photograph at a sensibly safe distance from the cheery-looking Gascoigne clan.

Thanks to his wonder-goal in Euro '96, Gazza's stock in July 1996 was at its peak. In the press, highbrow writers like Germaine Greer and A.S. Byatt were recruited to brood on the components of his genius and to analyse his popular appeal. Many a Rangers fan must have feared that Gascoigne would do to Scotland what he had done to Aberdeen, but there were few recriminations when he turned up for his second Ibrox season. Again hopes were sky-high. This surely would be Rangers' year in Europe, even though Ajax and Auxerre would have to be settled with along the way. And there was an extra spur this year in the domestic league. Celtic held the Scottish record for successive League championship titles: nine in a row. If Rangers could succeed once more in 96/97, they would equal this thought-to-be-unequallable record. And, it must be said, if the Ibrox fans had been asked to choose between winning the European Cup and chalking up nine titles in a row, they would almost certainly have opted for the local triumph. Maybe this was what was wrong with Rangers.

As it transpired, the fans got what they wanted: a ninth Scottish championship. They also collected yet another severe drubbing in the European League: a four-goal defeat by Ajax and even a three-nil trouncing by Grasshoppers of Zurich. Gascoigne, serving a two-match ban on account of last year's Dortmund sending-off, was absent for the opening defeats. And when he did return, he blew it yet again. Against Ajax, he kicked out at Winston Bogarde after a mere half an hour of play and got himself sent off. For Gazza, another European ban; for Rangers, another year of humbling self-appraisal. 'I'm disgraced', said Gascoigne, 'It happened last year and I said to the gaffer that it would not happen again. I've let down everyone at the club'.

Often enough, Gascoigne's conduct on the field of play – his near-invisible off days, his bursts of aggression, his over-the-top petulance – could be traced back to the current state of his relationship with Sheryl. Bad Sheryl days were usually marked by set-backs on the pitch. And this Ajax sending-off was no exception, as we discovered on the morning after Gazza's 'Dutch disgrace'. There was Sheryl, all over the front page of the *Daily Mirror*, her face bruised and puffy,

left arm bandaged, fingers in plaster. The headline read:
GAZZA BEATS SHERYL BLACK AND BLUE. The player, as
usual, was abject: 'I deeply regret what happened with my
wife', he said, 'It will live with me forever'.

And so it should, was the response from women's groups
and from various canvassed individuals like Julie Burchill,
Joan Bakewell and Rabbi Julie Neuberger. Gascoigne
should be punished in some way – but how? Certainly
he should never again be chosen to represent his country.
England had just appointed Glenn Hoddle as successor to
Terry Venables and the new manager was on the brink of
picking England's squad for the difficult World Cup
qualifier against Georgia. For several days after Gascoigne's
Sheryl shame, Hoddle was subjected to a bombardment of
advice – from bishops, opinion pollsters and numerous
features page philosophers – and most of it was virulently
anti-Gazza. At last his soccer delinquent had done something which could not be filed away under 'Laddishness' or
'Mischief'. Glenn, though, was a 'committed' Christian and
liked to think he knew a thing or two about salvation.
Gascoigne was selected for the Georgia game and Hoddle
postscripted his announcement with a heart-warming ser-
monette: 'One of the prime examples that Jesus spoke about
was forgiveness, in the long term, not just the short term.'
He did not 'condone' the player's conduct: 'I have high
standards', he assured us. At the same time though, 'I accept
that people are human. If Joe Public had done exactly the
same thing, that man wouldn't have got the sack and his
capacity to earn would not have been taken away from
him.' The Football Association 'fully backed' their manager's decision. 'We don't condone unacceptable beha-

viour', said Graham Kelly, the F.A.'s chief executive, 'We condemn it. We have some knowledge of personal matters that relate to the situation and we are convinced that Glen Hoddle's decision is the right one'. What was being hinted here? That Sheryl in some way *deserved* it? Surely not. At Bisham Abbey, just before the Georgia game with Hoddle at his side, Gascoigne offered further apologies and the manager once again pleaded for forgiveness. Gascoigne, said Hoddle, 'is hitting his prime. If he can get his personal life together, we could see a Paul Gascoigne nobody has seen yet. That would be fantastic. He will have to adjust his game. There are moments of magic he can still conjure up, and although these might be less frequent, he can be part of the jigsaw in many other ways.'

And this, of course, was what we Gazza fans had been hoping to hear. In spite of Ajax, in spite – even – of Sheryl, a long-term, in-the-round commitment, a near-promise that Glenn would stick with Gazza all the way to the World Cup. This was, perhaps, no more than we expected: after all, Glenn Hoddle would be the frist – would he not? – to recognise the fragility of Gascoigne's soccer genius. At the same time, though, Hoddle the manager was not the same as Hoddle the player. His Christian rectitude could easily have tempted him to take a harder line. But no, there was a touch of the scoutmaster in Glenn Hoddle: if one of his troop faltered, it was his job to see that the boy got back in line. He did not need to be told how. And he hoped, presumably, that the miscreant would remember who had saved him. On the whole, though, thank goodness for forgiveness: it seemed that we could at last look forward with confidence to Gazza doing the business in France '98.

At Bisham Abbey, towards the end of the press conference, an Italian journalist asked Hoddle: 'If Gascoigne became an ordinary person, would he also become an ordinary player?' A key question but Glenn's reply could not be faulted: 'I don't know. We do not have a crystal ball to look into. Paul has been given a gift from an early age but many things have clogged him. If we can release them, he could yet show that there is another Paul Gascoigne even better than in his heyday at Tottenham.'

In the wake of the Sheryl-beating scandal (and her subsequent divorce moves), the tabloids hounded Gazza with renewed ingenuity and purpose. They could now pose as the champions of Britain's battered wives. In March 1997, Gascoigne, we learned, was being 'questioned by detectives' about yet another 'alleged assault'. The victim this time was a fan of Gazza's friend, Chris Evans, the radio and TV star. When she approached Evans in his limousine outside the Cafe Royal, who should appear through the sunroof but Paul Gascoigne, who had 'punched her in the face'. In fact, those detectives never got to question Gazza. Immediately after the 'assault' he took off for a two week 'rest break' in New York, where he caused another stir by showing up to watch an Old Firm match in one of the city's Irish pubs. Worse still, he showed up wearing Celtic's colours.

For Rangers, this – far more than the alleged assault – was close to being the last straw. Gascoigne had been given this time off in New York in order to 'recuperate' from an injury he had managed to pick up in a friendly match in Holland, an injury which many observers thought could easily have been avoided. And now this Old Firm jest: didn't

Gascoigne know by now that hating Celtic was *not* funny?
At Ibrox, Walter Smith was beginning to sound like Sergio
Cragnotti. Smith had been upset by the Sheryl-beating
incident and spoke now of there being more to Gazza than
mere daftness. There was, he said, a 'darker, deeper side':

> Every time something happens with him I feel it myself.
> Believe me, there have been many times when I've sat
> down and thought I'd made a mistake. These off-pitch
> incidents can only happen so many times to one
> person, whether it's me or the previous management.
> When I signed him, I was 100 per cent clear about my
> judgement, but the percentage drops with every in-
> cident that happens. And so too does the level of
> backing at the club.

This reproof from the kindly and forebearing Smith hit
Gazza hard. There were regular reports of drinking jags
with Evans, his new pal. And Sheryl had announced that she
would shortly be filing for divorce – proceedings would
begin, she said, on July 1st, the couple's first wedding
anniversary.

Glenn Hoddle continued to back Gascoigne but even
with him the quality of mercy was beginning to look
somewhat strained. Although '75 per cent of what you hear
about Paul is fiction', Hoddle acknowledged that 'there are
some things he needs to change in his life. It is partly to do
with the mental side of things. He has to realise that you
can't do at 30 the things you used to get away with when
you were 21'. Was this a reference to the reported drinking
jags, or to Gazza's association with showbusiness types like

Evans? Hoddle was quite ready to be Gazza's mentor but he had no wish to share the job with a disc jockey. In another interview, just before announcing his squad for the World Cup qualifier against Poland, Glenn once again seemed less than fulsome when questioned about Gazza: 'I don't think there are many players better than Paul when he's at his best. But when was he at his very best? That's the question.' Even so, he picked Gascoigne for the squad. Again, though, there were troubling admonitions: Gazza had to get completely fit, change his 'life-style', and altogether 'start loving the game of football again.'

Gascoigne was injured in the away triumph against Poland but against Moldova and in the vital 0–0 draw with Italy in Rome he was, as Hoddle said, 'as good as he has been for a long time'. The draw in Rome clinched England's qualification for the World Cup finals and afterwards Hoddle was more relaxed than he had been for several months. England was going to France; Gascoigne had yet again delivered when it mattered. The prospects, for all concerned, seemed limitless. Hoddle was now basking in the critics' praise: he had been right, they said, to stick to Gascoigne. Glenn agreed. He put it down to fellow-feelings. 'I was always being told it was my last chance. I've learned from that how to treat Paul.'

And this continued to be the message, more or less, all the way through to the eve of the World Cup. Gascoigne, it seemed, had heeded his wise manager's advice and, when it was rumoured that he was likely to be leaving Rangers before the end of the current season (a season of failure, as it turned out, with Celtic winning what would have been Rangers' tenth title in a row, an all-time record), there were many who believed that Glenn had played some significant part in the decision. He wanted Gazza back in England, it was said. Gascoigne himself denied this and, in any case, Ranger's new manager-to-be, Dick Avocaat (Smith having been moved upstairs, like Dino Zoff), was making it clear that Gascoigne did not 'figure in his plans' for the next season.

Whatever the truth of the matter, Gascoigne – in March 1998 – changed clubs again. He signed for Middlesbrough, just in time to play a part (a depressingly small part, as it happened) in his new club's defeat by Chelsea in the Coca Cola Cup final. In this game, and in a handful of further games for Middlesbrough before the season's end, Gascoigne was sadly unimpressive – wearily peripheral most of the time, but easily exasperated when his one or two attempted tricks did not come off. Glenn Hoddle must have watched these games with some dismay. Even so, in every public statement he made during May 1998, Glenn allowed us to believe that Gascoigne, come what may, would almost certainly be in his final squad. When Gazza was photographed eating kebabs in Soho and then, two nights later, emerging – fairly blotto – from a restaurant in Notting Hill, Hoddle was reproving but still confident that he, Hoddle, could get Gazza back onto the straight and narrow. In the last week of May, when England's squad of thirty would be assembling in Spain, the whole question of Gazza's fitness would be seen to. At the time of Kebabgate, as the papers took to calling it, Gascoigne was 40 per cent short of match fitness, Hoddle said. The World Cup finals would begin on June 10, and England's first game was on the 15th. Before that the England team would be playing warm-up games against Belgium and Morocco. There was plenty of time, Glenn seemed to think, for Gazza to get fit.

The press did not agree. Day after day in the three weeks leading up to England's warm-up games the papers were full of Gazza stories: Gazza eats fatty foods; Gazza gets drunk in 'fashionable' restaurant; Gazza smokes twenty cigarettes a day. Gascoigne's response to this near-vendetta was defiant: he made jokes about kebabs and when he appeared on Chris Evan's Friday night TV show he merrily allowed the host to fill his mouth with cigarettes. When asked about the England squad, he simply said: 'If I'm in, I'm in; if I'm out, I'm out'. In other words, he was pretty sure that he'd be in.

And so were we, and so were most commentators, even the most hostile. And so too was Glen Hoddle, right up to the last minute. He picked Gazza for the warm-up games and continued to predict that the player's fitness would improve now that he was under the team coach's direct jurisdiction. Gascoigne did not play well in the warm-up games but neither did anybody else. As a team, England – like Gascoigne – seemed to be in need of extra training.

The drama of Gascoigne's expulsion from the Engalnd squad probably began during these warm-up games. Hoddle, it is rumoured, began to criticise the player's fitness face to face, much more directly than when he was talking to the press, and Gascoigne did not take kindly to such lectures. And Gazza's temper, we now know, was not improved by the stories he was hearing about Sheryl. On 28th May, three days before Hoddle was scheduled to announced his final twenty-two, the *Sun* ran a piece about Sheryl and her new 'Rugby hunk' boyfriend. Gazza, the *Sun* made clear, would not be made happy by the news that his 'estranged wife' (the divorce had not yet happened) had spent a long weekend in a Birmingham hotel with '6ft 3ins Gavin Batey', a Rugby-playing, forklift driving, part-time model. Pictures of the two romancers were supplied, under the heading GAZZA'S SHEZZA HAZZA NEW PAL CALLED GAVVA. Small wonder that Gascoigne was not in the mood for Hoddle lectures. On the night before Hoddle announced his twenty-two, the England players were permitted one night of 'relaxation' in the bar of their hotel in Spain. Gazza, as he would later confess, got very drunk. Did he on this same night en-counter Hoddle on the hotel stairs? Were words exchanged? Did Gascoigne perhaps allow himself a joke or two about faith healers? On the following day, May 31st, Gazza was out on the golf course with his team-mates, fooling around and still knocking back the lager. Glenn, meanwhile, was back in the hotel, studying videos of England's last two games, the warm-up games in which Gascoigne had been slow and sluggish. (In the second game, against Belgium he had got injured early on and had to be replaced.)

When, later this same day, Hoddle told Gascoigne that he ws excluded from the final twenty-two, the player 'went berserk' (Gascoigne's own words, but confirmed by Hod-dle's World Cup diary): 'I can't even begin to describe the hurt I feel', he told the *Sun*, 'Glenn Hoddle has destroyed my biggest dream'. On arriving back in England, he made straight for Sheryl's house and next day the couple flew off to Florida, leaving Gazza's dad to denounce Hoddle as a 'liar'. There were questions in Parliament, statements from Gordon Brown and William Hague, an extended edition of *Newsnight* and acres of equivocal newsprint. Nobody had quite expected this. After all, it was pointed out, Hoddle could have kept Gazza on the bench and used him sparingly or not at all. There was not need for this public banishment. Was there some thin-lipped satisfaction in Hoddle's demeanour when, at a press conference, he insisted that he had made a 'purely football decision – the player was not fit'? I do hope not. Even so, there was surely something disingenuous in Hoddle's 'what's all the fuss about?' response to those who pressed him for more detail. He knew very well what the fuss was about, and he also knew how Gascoigne must be feeling. 'I shall miss him', he asserted in one interview – but would he? Gascoigne has been the oldest player in his charge and the only one who had experience of the World Cup. He was closer in age to Hoddle than to Michael Owen, and for the young players in the squad he was a kind of soccer god. They had been in their early teens when Gazza shed his Turin tears. Of Hoddle's achievements as a player, these youngsters knew little beyond what they'd read or seen on TV clips.

It was a sorry ending. Would England have had a better World Cup if Gazza had been playing? This is not quite the point: we wanted Gazza in the team not just for England's sake. But yes, I think that he would probably have made an important difference in the slow-paced match against Romania. And he would certainly have scored in the shoot-out against Argentina (except that England would not have been playing Argentina if they had not lost to the Romanians). We'll never know, of course. And this, perhaps, is what we most resent: Glenn Hoddle's icy pragmatism has thwarted our hunger for, shall we say, the accidents of narrative. His was a prose decision and our disappointment, so we like to think, partakes of the poetic. Simply on aesthetic grounds, Gascoigne's exclusion from the 1998 World Cup was a calamity.

And yet it did deliver one poetic image. On the night of the Argentina game, with the whole nation glued to its TV screens, Gascoigne travelled alone by train from King's Cross to Newcastle. And, of course, nobody on the train knew who he was. On arriving at Newcastle's railway station, he joined the queue for taxis. Indeed, according to an eye-witness, he gave up his place in the queue to an 'old lady' who was struggling with her luggage. Humble, unrecognised, a proper gent: this was England's best foot-baller on the night of England's most important match since July 1990. Alas, though, the 'eye-witness' was a reporter from one of the tabloids. He accosted Gascoigne and began quizzing him about the Argentina game, which had just ended. What were his feelings now that England too had been expelled from France? Gascoigne dismissed him with a joke: since when did railway trains have TV aerials? The tabloid man backed off. Six weeks ago he would almost certainly have been given a good smacking.

It sounds corny – but then, with Gazza, what isn't corny or near-corny? Could it be that our hero had been trans-figured by disaster? Could it be that Glenn's bitter alchemy had worked? Perhaps Gascoigne was already focused on the Way Ahead – a new, slim, sober, caring-for-old-ladies Way Ahead that leads, or could lead, if this magic lasts, to Euro 2000? Now wouldn't that be something: the real Gazza, at long last, in top form for the millennium . And why not? After all, in 2000, Gascoigne will only be – what? – thirty three. The best, perhaps, is yet to come.